The Orphans

Los Huérfanos

by Lori Ortiz

ISBN: L 978-1-7329320-0-5

www.SycaMoorHomestead.com

This book is dedicated to my father,
Alfred Ortiz, son of Ramon Ortiz

CONTENTS

Some Spanish words are used in this book. Here is how to pronounce them and what they mean.

Abuelita	ah-bwel-EE-tah	Grandma
Adobe	ah-DOH-beh	Brick made from soil
Agave	ah-GAH-veh	Type of tall plant
Alameda	ah-lah-MEH-dah	A broad avenue
Ay!	AH-ee	Oh!
Boliche	boh-LEE-cheh	Type of toy
Burrito	boo-REE-toh	Meat or beans wrapped in a tortilla
Burro	BOO-roh	Donkey
Cajeta	cah-HEH-tah	Type of caramel candy
Calesta	cah-LEH-stah	Type of wagon
Campesino	cahm-peh-SEE-noh	Country folk
Cantina	cahn-TEE-nah	A bar
Caramba!	cah-RAHM-bah!	Drat!
Casa	CAH-sah	House
Centavo	sen-TAH-voh	A small coin
Chihuahua	chee-WAH-wah	A city in Mexico
Chile	CHEE-leh	A spicy pepper
Chorizo	choh-REE-soh	Type of spicy meat
Churros	CHOO-rohs	Sweet fried bread, similar to a donut
Cucaracha	coo-cah-RAH-chah	Cockroach
Dios	dee-OHS	God
Don	DOHN	Polite way to address a man
Empanadas	ehm-pah-NAH-dahs	Tiny pies
Enchiladas	ehn-chee-LAH-dahs	Fried stuffed tortillas
Fiesta	fee-EHS-tah	Party
Flan	FLAHN	Type of custard
Hacienda	ah-see-EHN-dah	Ranch
Hijito	ee-HEE-toh	Dear son
Hijo	EE-hoh	Son
Hola	OH-lah	Hi
Huarache	wah-RAH-cheh	Sandal
Idiota	ee-dee-OH-tah	Stupid person
Jesusita	heh-soo-SEE-tah	A woman's name
Lechugilla	leh-choo-GEE-ah	Palm tree roots containing a soapy substance
Mama	mah-MAH	Mom
Mantilla	mahn-TEE-yah	Type of shawl
Mariachi	mah-ree-AH-chee	Street musician
Menudo	meh-NOO-doh	Type of soup
Meoqui	meh-OH-kee	A village in Mexico
Mi	MEE	My
Mio	MEE-oh	Mine

Mira!	MEE-rah!	Look!
Mocoso	moh-KOH-soh	Child with a runny nose
Molcajeta	mohl-kah-HEH-tah	Stone bowl for grinding food
Mole poblano	MOH-leh poh-PLAH-noh	A type of sauce
Muchacho	moo-CHAH-choh	Boy
Muchas gracias	MOO-chahs GRAH-see-ahs	Thank you very much
Niñito	neen-YEE-toh	Little boy
Nopales	noh-PAH-lehs	Edible parts of a cactus plant
Ocotillo	oh-koh-TEE-yoh	Type of tall skinny bush
Padre	PAH-dreh	Priest; Father
Pan de leche	pahn deh LEH-cheh	Type of sweet bread
Papá	pah-PAH	Dad
Patio	PAH-tee-oh	Stone or tiled terrace
Peso	PEH-soh	A large coin
Piñata	peen-YAH-tah	A popular party game
Piñon	peen-YOHN	Edible seed of a pine tree
Plaza	PLAH-sah	Outdoor gathering place
Polícia	poh-LEE-see-ah	Police
Primícias	pree-MEE-see-ahs	First fruits; Tributes
Pulque	POOL-keh	Type of alcoholic drink
Ristras	REES-trahs	Strings of chile
Señor	sehn-YOR	Mr.
Señora	sehn-YOR-ah	Mrs.
Señorita	sehn-yor-EE-tah	Miss
Serape	seh-RAH-peh	Type of cloak
Sí	SEE	Yes
Sierra	see-EHR-ah	Mountain range
Sombrero	sohm-BREH-roh	Hat
Tacos	TAH-kos	Meat placed in a tortilla
Tamale	tah-MAH-leh	Steamed meat and dough
Tequila	teh KEE-lah	Type of alcoholic drink
Tía	TEE-ah	Aunt
Tío	TEE-oh	Uncle
Tortilla	tohr-TEE-ah	A thin flat bread
Vaya con Dios	VAH-yah kohn dee-OHS	Go with God
Villa	VEE-yah	Home of a wealthy person
Viva!	VEE-vah!	Live! (a popular cheer)
Yucca	YOO-kah	Type of flowering plant

Chapter 1

A FESTIVAL IS COMING

"MAYBE there will be fireworks!"

Luís was excited, chattering happily as he played among the bushy cactuses, while nearby his older brother Ramon and cousin Josefita sat digging in the ground for the roots of *yucca* plants. Luís's feet, in their brown *huarache* sandals, made crunching noises in the stony yellow sand.

"I heard Señor García is going to throw candy from his donkey-cart," said Josefita. She stood, her warm red dress heavy with the thick roots she'd collected, and went to dump her load into Ramon's basket.

"I'll be sure to catch some for us!" replied Luís. "Maybe Papá will even give us money to buy some *churros!* What do you think, Ramon?"

Ramon said nothing for a moment.

With a quick thrust of his knife, he cut the starchy root away from the tough plant and tossed it into the basket, trying to ignore the growling of his empty stomach. These roots they were gathering were all his family would be eating for supper tonight. Ramon Ortiz and his brother Luís were very poor.

This part of Mexico was all desert, and it was hard for anyone to earn a living. Some people had small ranches, or ran shops in the city of Chihuahua. Others, like their *mamá*, worked for these people, trying to make enough money to feed their own families.

But Luís was right. Tomorrow was New Year's Eve. And not just any New Year's Eve, but the end of a whole century. 1899 was about to end. Then it would be 1900! Even Ramon's hungry belly couldn't dampen his excitement. He looked up at Luís and grinned.

"Maybe he'll even come with us!"

"I'm going to wear my new *mantilla* that Tío Hector sent me," declared Josefita.

Everybody in Chihuahua had been talking for days of how they'd be celebrating the turn of the new century. There would be music, and dancing, and people selling toys and food.

It would be wonderful to see. Of course, Ramon knew that without money he and Luís would not be able to buy anything. But they could still enjoy the music, and wander through the streets looking at beautiful things for sale.

"Do you think Mamá will come?" Luís was asking.

"No, she has to go clean Señora Flores's house," answered Ramon. It was too bad, he thought. Mamá worked so hard she never had time to enjoy herself. She was always busy keeping house, sewing, and doing laundry for people in town, even cleaning for Padre Ochoa at the cathedral every week. But since Papá spent all his time drinking and gambling in town, there was only Mamá to earn any money for food.

Josefita was lucky. She had an uncle in America who sent money and gifts to Josefita's family. Last week for Christmas she had gotten a doll, a dress, and a beautiful lacy white *mantilla* with long fringe on it. All that Ramon and Luís had received Christmas morning were plain white shirts Mamá had made for them. They would have to last until next Christmas when Mamá would make them each another one.

Ramon wished he could go to America. Everybody there was rich! They had so much food to eat that they all got fat, and so many clothes to wear that they needed special rooms called closets just to keep them in.

He'd seen a picture once of America. The buildings there were taller than the cathedral steeple in town, much taller. They stretched up into the sky! All of the people living in Chihuahua could fit into just one of those huge buildings.

Ramon reached up to pull the brim of his round woven *sombrero* lower on his head to keep the setting sun off his face. It was growing late, and the shadows of the *yuccas* and the skinny *ocotillo* bushes around them were stretching out over the sand. And it was getting cold.

"Come on, Luís, we need to be going now." Ramon shrugged into his warm *serape* and strapped his basket over his back, and waited as his brother picked up the other basket. Josefita shook bits of gravelly sand out of her dress, and together the children headed back over the desert into the city.

The sun was nearly gone by the time the boys had thanked their cousin for her help and turned into Toro Alley where they lived. They walked past brown *adobe casas*, many with *ristras* of red *chile* hanging from the roofs to dry, and chickens and *burros* scuffling about in the dusty yards.

"Mamá! Mamá!" Luís went running into the *casa*, pattering across the earthen floor with his basket of roots, while Ramon pulled shut the door.

Just then Ramon smelled a delicious aroma coming from the stove in the corner. Beans! Mamá had cleaned for Señora Mendoza today, and the nice lady must have given some beans to Mamá. Too bad they had no pork meat to add, or even rice or *tortillas* to eat with it. Ramon grimaced, remembering that he and Luís still had to peel and slice the *yucca* roots before they could be fried.

Ramon carefully hung his straw *sombrero* and his *serape* on the wooden peg behind the door, pausing to make the sign of the cross over his breast as he passed Mamá's small statue of the blessed Virgin Mary, mother of Jesus. He joined Luís and Mamá at the stove on the other side of the room. Mamá looked very tired as she turned to give him a hug.

"*Hola, mi hijo,*" she said, ruffling his black hair. "Did you have a good day at school today?"

"*Sí*, Mamá." Ramon had only recently begun attending school. He enjoyed learning the alphabet and was already nearly caught up to the other children in the class. "Don Terrasus says I'll be ready to begin reading soon."

Picking up a knife, he carried his basket over to the table and sat down. “He’s giving us the day off from lessons tomorrow so we can go to the festival all day long.”

“Mamá, can you come with us to the festival? Please say you can,” interrupted Luís, clambering into a chair beside Ramon and looking up hopefully.

Mamá gave him a sad smile as she stirred the beans. “Luís, you know I have to work tomorrow. But you and your brother will have much fun on your own, I’m sure. *Dios mio*, it will be a day you will remember for your whole life! A new century happens only once every one hundred years. I wish I could be there with you.”

She whacked her spoon briskly against the pot. “But we have no more money. Señora Mendoza told me today that she cannot pay me until next week, so she gave me the beans instead.” She set the spoon down and wiped her hands on her apron, and looked at Ramon. “You are going to have to go and find your *papá*.”

Ramon paused in his peeling and scowled. He knew where he would find his *papá*. Drunk at the *cantina* in town.

Gathering up the sliced roots, he went to the stove and tossed them into a skillet, trying to remember if his *papá* had ever even lived with them. So far back as he could recall, Papá would come to the house to visit them, sometimes bringing food with him, occasionally even meat. One Christmas he had even brought with him a *boliche*, a small wooden cup with a ball on a string, as a gift for Ramon.

But afterward he always went away again, back to the *cantina* where he won money gambling and then spent it drinking *pulque* and *tequila*.

"Someday," said Ramon, tossing out the *yucca* peelings as Mamá served the beans, "we are going to be rich. We are going to live in America and have all the food and money we could ever need. And I will buy you a beautiful dress to wear."

Mamá smiled. "Ramon, you are such a dreamer."

But Ramon said nothing. This was one dream he was determined would come true.

Chapter 2

CHIHUAHUA CITY

"WATCH out, watch out!" Ramon yanked Luís out of the way as a big horse-cart turned into the narrow street. Scarcely noticing his close call, Luís stood, staring, as the cart continued on its way.

"But it's so beautiful!" Luís pointed at the cart as it vanished into the crowd of people.

Ramon took his brother firmly by the hand and led him along, silently agreeing with him. The cart *had* been beautiful. Its driver had painted bold, colorful flowers all along the sides of it, and its large wooden wheels were a deep blue. Best of all were the bright ribbons that fluttered in the horse's mane and tail. Ramon had never seen anything like it before.

As they joined the crowd, they could hear the sounds of much excitement. People were laughing and shouting, clanging bells and blowing on horns. Further ahead a group of *mariachi* singers in dazzling silver-stitched suits were playing music, their violins, guitars, and trumpets loud and vibrant in the morning air. The smells of roasting corn, sweet frying *churros, chorizo* meat, and other aromas swirled all around.

“Look! What do those say?” Luís was pointing now at the signs some people were holding up.

Ramon squinted at the signs. “That’s an ‘H’, and that’s an ‘A’, and I think that’s a ‘P’. . .” He gave it up. Naming letters was not the same as being able to read. “We can ask Josefita to read them to us. Come on!” He tugged at Luís’s hand. “She said she’d meet us on the Alameda.”

“Are we going to go find Papá now?”

“No.” Ramon was firm. “First we find Josefita, so she can watch you while I go into the *cantina*.”

“I don’t see why I can’t go into the *cantina*, too,” sulked Luís as he tried to keep up with Ramon.

“You know Mamá would not like you going inside there. Men gamble and get drunk and fight, and the women. . .” Ramon wasn’t sure what the wo-men did that was so bad, but one thing he did know: Mamá would be very angry if he let Luís go there.

He and Luís pushed their way through the crowd, past men and women with carts filled with things for sale.

“Limes! Fresh limes!” called one.

"Serapes! Huaraches! Sombreros!" called another, the sandals and hats hanging from a pole beside him and the colorful wool *serapes* draped over the sides of the cart.

One woman was selling brightly colored dresses and *mantillas*. Ramon gazed wistfully at them as he hurried past, but a dress for Mamá would have to wait for another day. They cost many, many *pesos*.

Just then somebody in the crowd shoved up against him, hard. Clutching more tightly at Luís's hand, Ramon looked to see who it had been. But there were too many people, all shoving and bumping each other in the general excitement.

In a crowd like this, he suddenly realized, there would be many pickpockets and other thieves, all hoping to steal something and not be noticed. It was something he had never really worried about before, since he rarely had anything to steal and had certainly never seen so many people all together, not even at Christmas. He would have to be careful, especially if Papá gave them any money.

With growing excitement, Ramon and Luís made their way toward the city center. Along the way they were joined by bicycles, their riders gaily calling out and ringing bells. More of the painted horse-carts passed them.

At last they came to the Alameda, a broad tree-lined avenue. It was filled with people, even more than had been in the street, and many of them were dancing to the bright music of more *mariachis* who were performing in the thin shade of cottonwood trees. Ramon's eyes grew wide as he saw several strange-looking items erected along one side. Fireworks! Oh, he could hardly wait for it to get dark. Tonight was going to be wonderful. He tugged excitedly at Luís's small hand.

"Ow, you're hurting me!" said Luís, pulling his hand from Ramon's. "Hey, look, there's Josefita." And before Ramon could protest, Luís had bolted away into the crowd.

"Luís!" Ramon ran after him, pushing his way through the crowd, trying to see where Luís had run. "Come back here!" He wove around the dancing people and past a man selling tin flutes until he saw his brother balancing atop a festive red cart of avocados, showing off to their cousin.

"Luís, get down from there! And don't run away like that." Ramon was panting as he joined them. Then he got a good look at Josefita and stared.

She was wearing one of the colorful ruffled dresses, all blue and gold, with lacy sleeves and stripes of red around the bottom. Her hair, usually tied into a single black braid, was caught up with ivory combs and hung brushed and sleek down her back. A delicate white-fringed *mantilla* draped over her head and about her shoulders, and on her feet were tiny shoes.

"Do you like it?" she asked, smoothing out the dress. "Papá bought it for me." Giggling, she twirled around. "Maybe we can dance later."

"You'll have to be careful not to get it dirty," said Luís, pointing to the puddles of mud out in the cobbled street.

"We're going to the *cantina* to find to our *papá*," explained Ramon as he led them away from the Alameda and down narrow roads. A man, hurrying by, bumped against Josefita, blew a tin horn into the air, and shouted "Happy New Year!" before continuing past.

There were even more people in the streets now than there had been before. People from nearby villages were arriving to join the festivities and to bring things to sell. They were mostly *campesinos*: farmers and ranchers dressed in simple white cotton like Ramon and Luís and leading *burros* with baskets strapped across their backs. Some *burros* carried women or children, eager to come see the city.

The *cantina* was noisy as always, with sounds of harsh laughter coming from inside, as well as the sounds of shouting and occasional breaking glass.

"I'll be right back," said Ramon, pushing open the door and leaving Luís and Josefita to wait for him outside.

But once inside the dark, noisy *cantina*, he quickly became dismayed. He had never seen the place so crowded! How was he ever going to find Papá among all these people? The room was packed with rowdy men celebrating the New Year. All of the tables were full, and more men were standing about, drinking *tequila* and cups of milky *pulque*. Many of the men wore daggers and some even had guns.

A loud smacking sound drew his attention over to the right, where a group of men were playing cards. One of them, evidently the loser, had angrily struck the table and then risen to his feet. Ramon took a step back. Was there about to be a fight? But Papá was not one of the card players, so Ramon turned aside and began to squeeze his way between groups of standing men.

Someone lurched against him and stepped on his foot. The next thing Ramon knew, warm liquid was pouring down the back of his neck, followed by the sound of a bottle smashing on the floor. "Hey, watch it, kid! Get outta here!"

Cringing, Ramon wormed his way through the crowd as fast as he could until he was flat up against the wall. He paused there to catch his breath and made himself look carefully at the faces of the men around him. Surely Papá was here. Maybe he was further back, seated at the bar.

Ramon left the wall to venture back out among the drunken men, ducking under a serving girl with a tray and making his way around the tables and back toward the bar. Sure enough, he spotted a familiar figure.

"Papá!" he said as he shoved his way over.

But Papá didn't answer. Papá was seated on a stool and slumped over the bar, clutching a bottle.

"Papá, wake up." Ramon plucked the bottle from Papá's hand and gently shook him, then tugged at his black beard. "Wake up, Papá, it's New Year's Eve and there's a big festival today and we want you to come with us."

But Papá just lay there.

"Luís is outside, and Josefita. They're waiting for us." Still nothing. Ramon shook him harder. "Please wake up."

It was no use. Papá was drunk, and Ramon knew he might not wake up all day.

But maybe he had some money.

It wouldn't really be stealing, Ramon thought, since Mamá had asked him to come get money from Papá. But it didn't matter, anyway, because when Ramon had shoved Papá over and dug his hands into Papá's pockets, they came out empty.

Nothing.

Angry shouts erupted from some men near Ramon, and one of them punched the other. The man staggered from the blow, then reached down for his gun. It was time for Ramon to leave.

He had just scrabbled his way back to the door when he heard the gunshot. Flinging open the door, he burst out into the sunshine and stood there blinking.

"What happened? Ramon, are you all right?" Luís and Josefita came hurrying up to him. "Was somebody shot?"

Ramon assured them he was fine. "That," he said to Luís, "is why Mamá doesn't like you going in there."

"But was Papá there? Did you find him? Is he going to come?"

"He was there, all right." Ramon was disgusted. "But he won't be coming with us." He took Luís by the hand and led him away from the *cantina.*

Luís licked his lips. "Did he give you any money?"

Ramon looked at his brother, then looked away.

"No."

The three children walked back toward the Alameda. It was difficult keeping together among all the people, but Ramon held Luís's hand tightly and Josefita stayed close.

The sun was high now and noon was approaching. It was getting hot, even though it was late December. Ramon and Luís adjusted their wide *sombreros* on their heads to shade their eyes from the sun, and Josefita wrapped her lacy white *mantilla* closely about her face.

They moved with the crowd, joining in the general gaiety, laughing and pointing and stopping from time to time to catch at the candies and novelties tossed from carts, or to admire the jewelry, woodwork, weavings, and other finery being peddled. Wooden toys, books, magazines, there were things for sale all up and down the road. Everywhere there was so much to see!

"What's that?"

Ramon looked to see where Luís was pointing. A group of older boys were gathered in a small circle, shouting and cursing and excitedly shoving each other as they watched something within the circle. Ramon could not see past them, but he heard loud squawks and saw a burst of colorful feathers fly into the air, accompanied by cheers and groans from the boys.

They were cockfighting, putting two roosters into a ring to fight each other. It was a very bloody sport, the roosters jabbing and cutting each other with their sharp leg spurs, often ripping off bits of flesh and sometimes even killing each other. Definitely not something Luís ought to see.

Naturally, Luís wanted to get closer. "Come on, Ramon, I want to go watch."

"Luís," said Josefita, "I really don't think you want to go over there." She, too, had seen the flying feathers.

Just then one of the gaily decorated carts came rattling along the cobbled street toward them, forcing people to move off to the side so it could pass. Painted in bright colors like the others had been, it was pulled by a big ox, and there were words printed on the animal's horns.

Glad for the distraction, Ramon tugged Luís away from the cockfighting and asked Josefita, "What do those horns say?"

His cousin squinted her eyes at the ox as it lumbered past, then pointed.

"That horn says '1899' and the other one says '1900'. And the sign hanging from the side of the cart says 'Goodbye Old Year! Hello New Year!'" She waved a cheerful greeting to the ox driver and he waved back to her as the cart slowly disappeared into the crowd.

The children continued strolling down the street along with everybody else, enjoying the festive colors, the music playing on every street corner, the enticing smells of cooking food, and the general air of celebration.

"Hot *tamales*! Get your hot *tamales* here!"

"*Burritos*! Bean *burritos*!"

"Chocolate! Hot *churros* here!" Ramon paused as they walked past to gaze longingly at the man dropping bits of dough into frying fat. Sweet sugary *churros*, and hot chocolate to drink, oh how Ramon wished he had some money to buy them.

"*Ay!* Stop thief!" A man selling mangoes from a cart was waving frantically. "That boy stole all my money! Stop him!"

Just then somebody slammed hard into Ramon, nearly knocking him down. Without thinking, Ramon wrapped his arm about his assailant and wrestled him to the ground.

"Let me go!" the other boy cried, struggling to free himself.

But the mango seller was hurrying over as fast as he could. "Yes, that's him. Don't let him go."

The man grabbed the thief by the arm, roughly dragging him to his feet.

"You will give me back the money you took from me, eh?" He wrenched a small pouch from the boy's grip. "Now scat, and be glad I don't turn you in to the *polícia.*"

Tying the pouch to his belt, the man shoved the boy away to disappear into the crowd, and then turned to Ramon.

"What quick wits you have, my son. I have you to thank for saving everything I have earned today. Here, I would like to give you something for what you have done."

Picking up a small sack, he filled it with mangoes and gave it to Ramon. "Here you go, son, and Happy New Year!"

With a wide grin, Ramon accepted the sack.

"Happy New Year to you, too, *señor*!" Wait till Mamá saw these! Ramon could hardly wait to show her.

"Ramon, Ramon, let me see!" Luís peered into the sack at the sweet, juicy mangoes. He reached a hand in to grab one.

Just then church bells began to toll. It was noon, and the *padre* was summoning everyone to come worship at Mass.

"We should go," said Josefita, and Ramon agreed. He knew it was important to attend Mass as often as they could. Many of the people in the streets also began to head toward the cathedral.

"Come on, Luís." Ramon put his brother's mango back into the sack. "We can eat afterward. Let's go to the cathedral."

Chapter 3

THE CONTEST

"*HOLA*, Josefita! Happy New Year!" A lady in a pretty green ruffled dress was calling to them from the city's Plaza de Armas as they left the cathedral an hour later.

"That's Señora Rodriguez," said Josefita. "I wonder what she wants. *Hola*, Señora!"

Señora Rodriguez came bustling over to them, towing a small boy along after her.

"I must talk with Señora Torres." She gestured to another lady, who was fanning herself in the cool spray of the *plaza's* great fountain. "But Pedro wants to see the festival. Will you take him with you for a while? We'll return for him here in an hour or so. Oh, thank you Josefita dear."

With that, she placed the boy's hand in Josefita's and hurried back to where Señora Torres waited, leaving the children to stare after her.

"I guess we're bringing Pedro with us," said Josefita.

"I suppose we are." Ramon was none too pleased. Pedro was even younger than Luís. "What do we do if he gets lost?"

"He won't get lost, will you, *hijito*," assured Josefita as they left the *plaza* and headed out into the street. "And if he does. . ." She paused a moment to kneel and look the small boy in the eye.

"Pedro, if you get lost, ask somebody to take you to the *plaza*. Do you understand? If you get lost you must go back to the *plaza* and wait there by the fountain, and we will come find you. Now take your thumb out of your mouth. Do you understand what I've just told you?"

"*Sí*, Josefita. If I get lost I am to ask somebody to take me to the *plaza*."

"Very good. Now hold my hand and you won't get lost."

After sharing a quick lunch of mangoes from Ramon's sack, the children rejoined the crowd and ambled along the street taking in the sights. The sun moved toward afternoon, and the sounds of music and laughter began to be joined by less wholesome sounds, such as shouting and an occasional fistfight. Nervously steering Pedro and Luís away from these, Ramon and Josefita found themselves leaving the crush of people and entering a deserted back alley.

An odd, metallic sound caught Ramon's attention, a sharp clanging noise. It came again, accompanied by the sound of hoots and derisive laughter.

"You couldn't hit the broad side of a barn!"

The clanging noises and the laughter were coming from a bare yard in the alley, where a pair of older boys were shooting rocks at tin cans stuck over the branches of a spiny *ocotillo* bush growing from the sand.

"Oh, yeah? I hit that can dead center and you know it!"

"Ha! You just clipped it, Diego. Lucky shot."

"It was not!" The boy Diego looked up then and saw Ramon and the others. "What are you staring at?" he demanded.

"Nothing," mumbled Ramon, shifting the awkward mango sack on his shoulder and motioning for his group to move away.

"No, wait," said the other boy. He gestured for Ramon to come back. "I have an idea." He turned to Diego. "Let's ask him to be the judge."

"Why?" said Diego. "You know I beat you. I can beat you any day, Mateo."

"What's the matter, Diego?" taunted Mateo. "Chicken?"

"Am not! OK, have it your way." Diego reached into his pocket and approached Ramon. "Here, kid." He pressed a coin into Ramon's hand. "Watch me and Mateo shoot, and then you can tell him I'm better than he is. Deal?" Diego glanced over at Mateo, who just shrugged.

Looking down at the coin, Ramon saw it was a five-*centavo* piece. Five *centavos* just to judge a shooting contest? Ramon could hardly believe his luck.

"Deal!"

He watched as the boys carefully set the two cans up in the *ocotillo* bush and then took turns shooting with their slingshots, knocking the cans to the ground. Fetching the cans from where they had fallen, Ramon examined them closely.

"This can was hit near the top. Here, you can see the dent where it was struck." He pointed. Then he studied the second can.

"This one was shot square in the center," Ramon handed it to Mateo, impressed. "It's yours, actually."

"What!" shouted Diego, growing red in the face. "That's impossible. It must be *my* can."

Ramon sensed that a fight was about to break out. Clutching at his sack, he fumbled for Luís's hand and began to edge away, nudging Josefita and little Pedro ahead of him.

"*Ay!* Come back here!" Diego grappled after Ramon, barely missing him. Ramon and the rest of the children ran as fast as they could out of the alley and back toward the festivities.

"Come back here with my money!" hollered Diego, giving chase while Mateo burst into laughter.

Wondering how he had gotten into this mess, Ramon quickly ducked back into the crowd, pulling the others along with him. A horse-cart came clattering past, causing Josefita to shriek as it missed them by inches.

Ramon scarcely even noticed the cart's bright painted colors or the horse's fluttering ribbons. Had Diego seen him? Ramon's heart was pounding as he scanned the faces of the people about him. No sign of the bully. *Ay, Dios mio*, that had been close! He breathed a sigh of relief at their narrow escape.

Only then did he realize he was still clutching the coin. His face lit up in a huge grin. Five *centavos*!

He sobered for a moment, wondering if he had, indeed, stolen it as the furious Diego seemed to think. But no, the big boys had agreed he should judge their shooting, and he had done so. It was not his fault that Mateo had been the better shot. Pocketing the coin, he decided that the next time he went to Mass he would confess this to the *padre*, in case it *was* a sin. But in the meantime. . .

"*Churros* and chocolate for everyone!"

Chapter 3

ONCE EVERY HUNDRED YEARS

RAMON was licking the last of the sugar from his fingers when he noticed Josefita was sitting alone. Puzzled, he asked, "Where's Pedro?"

Josefita glanced about, growing alarmed.

"He's gone!"

"Pedro! Pedro!"

They were seated on the gritty ground beside a tough, green *agave* plant, where they had carried their treats so they could eat and watch the crowd go by.

"When was the last time you remember seeing him?" asked Ramon.

"I gave him some of my chocolate to drink and told him not to burn himself." Josefita pointed. "Look, there's the cup."

The tin cup sat, empty, wobbling slightly in the rocky sand near her feet.

"He's got to be nearby," Ramon assured her. "Here, Luís." He handed his brother the second cup. "Finish drinking this and go return them to the man." Standing up, Ramon began calling out again. "Pedro!"

"Look," said Josefita. "I'll bet he went over there."

On a street corner ahead of them, some people had gathered to watch a man juggling balls in the air. Gesturing impatiently to Luís, Ramon followed Josefita to see if Pedro was among them.

"He's not here. Oh, where can he have gone?"

"Don't worry, Josefita. I know where he'll go." Ramon motioned for the others to follow him. "Remember, you told him if he gets lost to meet us at the *plaza*."

"By the fountain. That's right!"

Clasping Luís's hand tightly, Ramon slung his sack over his back and led Luís and Josefita through the merry people in the streets and past the horse-carts, ox-carts, and *burro*-carts that were more and more beginning to crowd the streets. "Happy New Year!" strangers cried to each other, blowing horns and tossing bits of paper into the air. The cobbled street was already littered with trampled confetti and torn streamers.

The Plaza de Armas was filled with even more people than before, many dressed in gay colors and others wearing the simple white of poor farmers, all celebrating and dancing to the music of *mariachis*.

"I still don't see him," said Josefita as they wormed their way over to the great fountain.

"What?" Ramon could not hear her above the lively music and the noise of so many people.

"I said I still don't see him. I don't think he's here."

"Wait a minute." Setting down his sack, Ramon walked over to a nearby palm tree. Grasping the rough trunk, he shinnied up and leaned out, carefully keeping his balance. From here, he could look down upon the faces of everybody beneath him.

Still no sign of Pedro.

With a worried sigh, he dropped back to the ground and shook his head.

"Here, take Luís." He nudged his brother over to Josefita. "Stay here in case Pedro comes."

"Where are you going?"

"Back to where we ate. He must still be there."

"But—"

"Just stay right here!" Ramon was adamant. "I'll be back." With that, he slipped away into the crowd.

Shoving his way through knots of people, he left the teeming *plaza* and returned to the equally teeming streets until he recognized the spot where they had all sat for their snack.

And there was Pedro.

The child, sitting patiently beside the stout *agave* plant, smiled and rose to his feet when he saw Ramon.

"I knew you'd come back," he said.

For a moment Ramon stood there, stunned.

"Where were you?" he demanded. "We went to the *plaza* but you weren't there. We told you if you got lost to go to there. Why didn't you?"

Pedro looked up at Ramon, puzzled.

"Because I wasn't lost."

"Huh?" Now Ramon was puzzled. "What do you mean? We looked up and you were gone."

"Sure. I went over there to watch the juggler. I came back and you were gone, so I sat down to wait. But I was never lost, I was right here the whole time."

Ramon rolled his eyes in disbelief. What a mix-up! "I guess we should have been more clear about what being 'lost' meant," he said with a grimace. "Here, climb up on my back. Josefita and Luís are waiting for us."

He knelt so the boy could scramble up, then stood and once again set out into the crush of merry-makers in the street, arriving breathless back at the *plaza.*

"Oh good, you found him." Josefita reached out to take the boy from Ramon. "His *mamá* was just here asking for him. I told her he was with you."

"And Josefita has to leave now, too," added Luís.

"*Sí*, Mamá and Papá are here and want me to come with them." Josefita gave Ramon a quick hug. "Maybe I will see you later tonight."

"We will be here. We don't want to miss the fireworks, do we, Luís?"

Josefita grinned. "Neither do I!"

"You'll take Pedro back to his *mamá*?"

"*Sí*, that's her standing right over there." She set the boy down on the ground and took his hand firmly in her own. Waving to Ramon as she turned to leave, she called out, "See you tonight, then!"

Ramon waved back. He could hardly wait until tonight.

"It's going to be fun, isn't it, Luís?" Ramon turned toward his brother.

But Luís was not there.

"Luís?"

Ramon couldn't believe it. This couldn't be happening again.

"Luís!"

Shouldering his way past people, Ramon searched about frantically.

The sound of laughter and shouts from a nearby alley drew his attention. A group of boys, mostly older, stood about, facing away from Ramon and intently watching something he could not see. Cockfighting, he was certain.

Then he groaned.

"Luís! What are you doing over there?" Hurrying to join him, Ramon grasped his errant young brother firmly by the shoulder and tried to pull him away. But Luís shook him off.

"No, Ramon, it's OK, see?" Luís pointed. "These nice boys said that if that rooster there," and Luís indicated a scrawny bird with matted green feathers trying to run away from a larger, meaner bird, "wins, then they will give him to me!"

Ramon shook his head. "Luís, Mamá will be very sad to learn you have been gambling."

"But I'm not gambling. I thought gambling was something men did with cards."

"And what did you tell these boys you would give them if your bird loses?"

Luís shrugged his shoulders. "I told them they could have my *sombrero*."

Just then a burst of jeering laughter from the boys made Ramon and Luís look in time to see the hapless rooster fall over dead.

One of the laughing boys reached over and snatched the *sombrero* from Luís's head, tossing it mockingly to his fellows as the surviving rooster was caught and stuffed into a sack.

Luís began to cry. "What do I do now, Ramon?"

Ramon thought very hard. "Wait a moment!" he called out to the boys. He had an idea, and hoped it would work. He pulled something from his pocket.

The *boliche* was a wooden cup about the size of an egg, set on a stick with a string and a small ball tied to it. It was a popular game among boys, to see how many times one could swing the ball into the cup without missing, and Ramon was the best of anyone in his class at school. He took it with him nearly everywhere he went so he could always practice.

"Which of you is best at this? I'll bet that I can beat you!" Now Ramon was making bets, too. He definitely hoped Mamá never found out about this!

The big boys stared at him, not quite sure what to make of this turn of events, then evidently decided that there was sport to be had here. Amid much ribald laughter, one slouching youth was shoved forward, clutching at a *boliche* of his own.

"I can beat you, *cucaracha*," he sneered.

Ramon tried to sound braver than he felt. "No, I will beat you. If you win, you can have my *sombrero*, too. But if I win Luís can have his *sombrero* back—and we also get the dead rooster. Do you agree?"

The boy spat on the ground and nodded his head once, then held up his *boliche*, ready to begin.

"Be ready to run, Luís, if this goes badly." Licking his dry lips, Ramon held up his *boliche* as well.

"Ready?" someone called. "And—*go*!"

"One! Two! Three! Four!" All of the boys, and Luís, too, were chanting excitedly as they watched the balls swinging on the ends of their strings, each one landing neatly into its cup to be tossed back out and swung again. Ramon, however, was not counting, concentrating only on making sure he did not miss. Click! Click! Click! Each click meant that the ball had landed in the cup, and that he was still winning. One miss, and he would lose. He must not miss!

"Thirty-three! Thirty-four! Thirty-five!"

Sweat began to mat Ramon's black hair and roll down his face. If it got in his eyes he would not be able to see. Gritting his teeth, he concentrated harder.

"Fifty-seven! Fifty-eight! Fifty-nine!"

Ramon was growing tired. He had never had to play for so long, most other boys his age having lost long before now. But his opponent must be getting tired, too, and this gave Ramon the encouragement he needed to continue.

"Seventy-two! Seventy-three!"

Just then, a sudden hot gust of desert breeze blew sand into Ramon's face. Blinking furiously, he swung the cup and heard the reassuring "click" of a successful catch.

Evidently the other boy had not been so lucky. The raucous counting had abruptly ceased, to be replaced by laughter and jeers.

"Ha, ha, Francisco lost to a little boy!" the youths taunted their mate. "Waaah, waaah, a baby beat Francisco!"

The gang began tussling with the unfortunate loser. Inching away, Ramon wondered what he should do. Although he didn't much care for being called a baby, he *had* won the game fair and square. Would the others try to make trouble for him?

But nobody seemed to be paying him any heed, caught up as they were in teasing their buddy. Gingerly, Ramon reached for Luís's *sombrero* where it had been tossed carelessly to the ground beside the dead rooster.

One of the boys looked up, and Ramon froze. But the boy waved a hand dismissively at Ramon and went back to the general horseplay. The game and its aftermath had been all but forgotten as the roughhousing youths moved along to go find excitement elsewhere, leaving Ramon and Luís alone in the small, quiet alley.

"You were great!" said Luís, beaming up at his older brother. "I've never seen you play for so long."

Grinning sheepishly, Ramon picked up the *sombrero* and placed it on Luís's small head, then put the limp rooster into his sack. With mangoes and chicken, they would eat well for the rest of the week, until Mamá could be paid.

"But," he wondered as he took Luís's hand and guided him back toward the festival, "how am I going to explain to Mamá where we *got* the rooster?"

Ramon and Luís spent the rest of the afternoon and evening scampering about the city, getting into mischief and grandly enjoying the holiday. The crowd continued to grow, and when the sun went down bonfires were lit about the Alameda, casting light upon the revelers. Exuberant people blew horns and waved signs, while shopkeepers handed out free calendars for the year 1900.

Amid the blaring music, the dancing, and the firelight, midnight gradually drew near, until finally it was time. All around Ramon, people rang bells, blew their horns, and shouted joyously.

From where he stood with Luís, he could see Josefita huddled excitedly with her parents. She waved to Ramon and he waved back. Someone threw confetti into the air. It scattered over Ramon, getting in his face and in his hair. The crowd began chanting, "Five! Four! Three! Two! One! *Happy New Year!*"

Ramon shouted, too, as the fireworks were lit, showering golden sparks into the air. Couples began dancing round and round amid the sparks, their faces lit up in the bright glow despite the dark of the night.

The *mariachis*, with their trumpets and violins, were playing Ramon's very favorite song, *Jesusita en Chihuahua*, a lively, bouncy song that made Ramon want to clap his hands. Other people began to clap, too, and soon Ramon, Luís, Josefita, her family, and everybody else were laughing and clapping and singing along.

> Yo ya me voy, ya me voy para Chihuahua.
> Ya me voy a buscar a mi linda Jesusita.

As the song came to an end, Ramon felt he had never been happier in his whole life.

"Happy New Year!" he whooped into the night. Once every hundred years, Mamá had said. A night like this would never happen again as long as Ramon lived. He hoped he would remember it always. "Happy New Year!"

Chapter 4

MOVING UP IN SCHOOL

THE March wind whistled and blew through cracks in the window and into the small classroom where Ramon and the other children were studying. It was spring now, nearly Easter, and the occasional storms that pelted the desert with rain and lightning had carpeted the barren ground with a rainbow of blooming cactuses.

Ramon leafed through the pages of his book. It was a small book Josefita had given him about the life of Saint Francis. A book of his very own! Ramon was terribly proud of it.

All winter long, Josefita had helped him study from it, pointing out the letters of the alphabet with a chicken quill, and then showing him how the letters together formed words.

Sometimes Josefita would give him a stick of charcoal and a board, and have him copy letters and words out of the book. She said this was how one learned to write. At first his writing was scrawled and clumsy, but gradually it improved until the teacher, Don Terrasus, had said that Ramon was ready to write in ink with a quill pen.

After that, Ramon could hardly wait to get to school each day. He shaved the quill of a chicken feather until it had a fine point, and would dip it into the inkwell that the class shared. *My* mamá *is beautiful,* he would write. *I love my* mamá. Or sometimes *I will go to America.* He practiced over and over until he could write in crisp, precise handwriting.

Just now he was copying a passage from his book. *St. Francis was a holy man who lived in Assisi, Italy.*

"Ramon?"

Looking up from his writing, Ramon saw that Don Terrasus was calling to him. Carefully setting down his quill and capping the inkwell, Ramon went to where the teacher sat at his desk at the front of the sunny classroom.

"Ramon, you're a very bright boy. You've learned quite a bit in the past few months."

"Thank you, *señor.*" Ramon was pleased that his hard work had been noticed.

"I'm going to promote you now to Don Jimenez's advanced class, where you will study arithmetic, geography, grammar, and Christian doctrine."

Ramon could hardly believe his luck. He would be in the big boys' class! Mamá was going to be proud of him.

He looked over at Josefita as he returned to his desk for his belongings. She smiled, and Ramon knew she was happy for him. He wished she could join him, but knew she would never be allowed in the advanced class. It was fortunate that her father had permitted her to attend school at all, for most girls stayed at home to help their mothers with housework.

"I'll see you after school," Ramon promised her, and she nodded eagerly.

Ramon walked out of the classroom and shut the door gently behind him. Don Jimenez's room was the next one over. Ramon could hear singing coming from there, in the high voices of boys. But as he nudged open the door, he stopped and stared, not quite believing what he saw.

By the window stood Don Jimenez, a stout wooden ruler clenched in his hand. And at the front of the class Ramon could see the boys, each kneeling painfully upon bricks as they sang.

"Jesu dulcis memoria dans vera cordis gaudia!" The words were Latin. *Jesus, the very thought of thee with sweetness fills the breast!*

Ramon had sung the beautiful hymn many times himself at Mass.

But why is he punishing them? Confused, Ramon took a step back, hoping the teacher had not yet seen him. He stumbled and bumped against the door, which gave a loud squeak. Don Jimenez looked up.

"You there!" The teacher pointed his ruler at Ramon. "What are you doing here?"

"I—"

"Speak up, boy!" Don Jimenez advanced upon Ramon, then whirled and struck the ruler forcibly upon the nearest desk. "Keep singing!" he shouted to the boys. "I did not say you could stop!"

Ramon took a deep breath. "I was sent here by Don Terrasus. He says I'm to be in your class now." He looked past Don Jimenez to where the kneeling boys had raggedly resumed their singing, and he shuddered.

Don Jimenez stood looking down at him for a moment, then turned and pointed with the ruler toward an empty desk. Without a word, the man strode to the front of the room where he idly cuffed the nearest boy before addressing the class.

"You may return to your seats, catechism is over. We shall now have our geography lesson."

With that, he pulled down a map in front of the blackboard.

The boys, groaning as they stood and rubbed at their knees, left the bricks and sat gratefully down at their desks.

"What was that?" Ramon whispered to the boy at the desk beside his.

The boy scowled. "That was catechism class, where we learn all about Jesus Christ and—"

Hot fire flared on Ramon's hand and he yelled in surprise. He had not seen Don Jimenez approaching, nor the heavy ruler that came smacking down.

"I can see already that we're going to have trouble with you." The teacher raised his ruler again and Ramon flinched, rubbing at his hand. "What is your name?"

"Ramon, sir."

"On your knees, Ramon! You will give me ten Our Father's, *now!*"

Bewildered, Ramon dropped to his knees and began to pray. "Our Father, who art in heaven. . ."

What kind of a class was this? He knew from Padre Ochoa at the cathedral that Jesus was kind and loving. But there stood Don Jimenez, his eyes blazing with fury. Ramon gritted his teeth. ". . .and lead us not into temptation, but deliver us from evil."

As the days went by, Ramon gradually grew used to the advanced class. Don Jimenez was quick to strike with his ruler, but he taught the boys well, and Ramon learned much that spring. He did especially well in arithmetic, often solving difficult math problems where the other boys could not.

He still played with Luís and Josefita after school, and even gave them short lessons based upon what he had learned in school, much as his cousin had done for him. Mamá continued to earn a living by cleaning for people.

The only bad news came from Padre Ochoa, who came often to the house to talk to Mamá. He told her how Papá's drinking had grown much worse. Mamá shrugged her shoulders. There was nothing she could do for the man, she said, except pray for him.

And this she did, kneeling late into the night before her statue of the blessed Virgin Mary, praying to the mother of Jesus to help Papá find peace.

Her prayers were answered, for one day the *padre* came to tell Mamá that Papá had been found dead in the *cantina*. He was with Jesus now.

Ramon hoped Papá was happy in heaven. Don Jimenez's grammar lesson the following morning faded away as Ramon gazed out the window, wondering what heaven must be like.

Smack! came the teacher's dreaded ruler upon Ramon's hand.

"Pay attention to the lesson, Ramon!"

"But my *papá*. . . I was thinking of my *papá*. . .

Smack! "You will not talk back to me!" Don Jimenez was very angry now, and struck Ramon's hand until red welts criss-crossed the skin.

"Oh, God!" Ramon cried out in pain.

"Yes, there is a God," snarled Don Jimenez, "but you don't fear him enough!" Cuffing Ramon hard on the head, the teacher sent him sprawling out of his seat onto the floor. "Go kneel at the front of the class, and as you kneel on those bricks, think of how Jesus Christ was nailed to a cross. He suffered to save sinners. Like you!" With a final clout, he sent Ramon scurrying forward.

As Ramon sank to his small, bony knees on the pile of bricks, he thought of what Padre Ochoa had told him not long ago. *You will soon be making your First Holy Communion,* the *padre* had said, *and it is important that you pray and do much penance to prepare your heart to receive the King of Heaven.* Ignoring the pain of the bricks, Ramon closed his eyes and began to pray.

Chapter 5

RAMON'S BIG DAY

RAMON peeled the sweaty shirt from his back and tried to concentrate on his prayers. It was June now, and so hot in the school that the classes had to take turns studying outside on the *patio*. The desert breeze ruffled Ramon's hair. A few feet away bees buzzed amid the creamy white blossoms of the *yucca* plants. The red-flowered bougainvillea hanging in the brick archway waved gently.

The shaded archway was the only cool place on the *patio* just now, and Don Jimenez dozed there, leaning against the wall with his *sombrero* pulled forward over his face. The older boys, snickering to themselves at their cleverness, were taking advantage of this by passing around a tiny bottle of *tequila* as they furtively leafed through a magazine one of them had smuggled in.

The stacked bricks were hard beneath Ramon's knees but he endured the pain silently, his lips moving only to repeat the words of the *Gloria* hymn. Indeed, he was so excited that he scarcely even felt the sharp bite of the bricks. The big day was almost here!

In two days he and some of the younger boys in Don Jimenez's class would be making their First Holy Communion. This was a very special day in the life of a child, for from this day forward he or she would be permitted to receive the Holy Eucharist each time they attended Mass.

Take this and eat it. Do this in remembrance of me. This was what the Bible said. *The King of Heaven will dwell in your heart*. This was what Padre Ochoa said.

It was important to make one's heart pure. Ramon squinted his eyes and thought very hard. Had he sinned recently?

The sun was high in the sky, and Ramon tugged at his *sombrero* so it shaded his face. The other boys in the First Communion class were kneeling beside him.

"I'm thirsty," one of them said.

"Shh!" said another. "The *don* might wake up and hear you."

"*Sí*, be quiet," said still another. "Remember, the wicked soldiers gave Jesus vinegar to drink while he was dying on the cross."

Ramon licked his lips. There would be water for them to drink when they returned to the classroom, not vinegar. But Roberto, the boy who had complained, came from a wealthy family and likely was not used to hunger or thirst. Even the clothes he wore were expensive. Ramon caught himself envying them and put a hasty halt to that thought. Envy was a sin!

Fortunately, on the evening before the ceremony there was a special Sacrament of Penance at the cathedral, where the boys could confess their sins and be forgiven.

When they arrived they were all lined up by a deacon, a tall man studying to become a *padre*, and told to wait until each had had a turn. One by one they went to kneel behind a curtain and confess their sins to the *padre*. Once each boy had come back out, the deacon would ring a little bell and the next boy would go in.

As Ramon waited nervously, he looked about at the dark cathedral. It smelled of lemons, beeswax, and fresh linens. Today had been Mamá's day to clean here, Ramon remembered, and he smiled. It was almost as if she were here with him now.

The bell sounded, and it was Ramon's turn. He had been to confession many times, but he never got over the quivery way he felt each time he walked behind the curtain. He had to tell the *padre* everything bad he had done. And what if he forgot something? Was that a sin, too?

"Bless me, *padre,* for I have sinned." Reciting the formal address, Ramon made the sign of the cross over his breast and bowed his head.

What had he done recently that might be a sin? "I disobeyed Mamá last week and climbed over a fence." He had fallen and ripped the knee of his trousers, which Mamá had stayed up late to mend. "Oh, and I was envious of Roberto's fine clothes," he remembered to add.

And then his confession was over and the *padre* was giving him the blessing. "Go and sin no more." Breathing a sigh of relief, Ramon pushed open the curtain for the next boy to enter.

When all the boys had finished, the deacon dismissed them. Making the sign of the cross over his breast with holy water, Ramon hurried home through the summer evening twilight.

"Mamá! Mamá!" he said as he pushed open the door of their *casa.* He could smell *enchiladas* cooking, and eagerly went in. Then he stopped short.

"It is all right *mi hijo*," said Mamá, turning from the stove to give him a hug. "Padre Ochoa is here to give you a gift."

It was the unfamiliar sight of the *padre* sitting at the family table that had confused Ramon. A holy *padre* in Ramon's own home. Was he supposed to kneel to greet the man? Bow? Speechless, he simply stood there.

The *padre*, as if sensing Ramon's perplexity, rose from the table and placed a bulky, brown-wrapped item into the boy's hands. A gift, Mamá had said.

"Your *mamá* is a very hard-working lady," he was saying. "She keeps the cathedral exceptionally clean, and it is always a pleasure to hear her praying or singing as she works."

Ramon looked up at that, surprised. Mamá, singing? She never sang around the *casa*. But then he realized the truth, that of course she would be too exhausted from her day's labors to have any energy left for singing at home.

As if she could read his thoughts, Mamá smiled and reached out to cup his chin in her hand so that he looked up at her.

"It is good to sing as you work, *mi hijo*. And to pray. It lightens the heart, and makes the load easier to bear." She returned to the stove where she was cracking eggs into a skillet and then sliding them one by one onto stacks of fried *tortillas.*

"And always remember," she continued as she placed the largest plate before the *padre* and set three smaller ones for herself, Ramon, and Luís, "that Jesus Christ Himself was a humble worker, a carpenter. There is no shame in hard work, and you must always do your best and not complain."

"She works hard," the *padre* repeated, while Mamá stepped out for a moment to call Luís. "But I know it has been very difficult for her, especially now with your *papá* gone. And so I wanted to help her by doing this small thing. Go ahead," he said, nodding at the package that Ramon stood holding. "Open it."

Still somewhat confused, but curious now as well, Ramon quickly untied the string and unwrapped the brown paper. Then he gasped.

Nestled within the paper was a suit, a real suit, all white and so fine and bright that Ramon was afraid to touch it.

Nor was this all. A pair of sleek black polished shoes reflected his astonished face.

"A boy's First Communion is a very special day," the *padre* explained.

Ramon's eyes shone with gratitude and he hurried to place the beautiful new clothes safely beside his bed. He could hardly wait till tomorrow!

He was up before the sun the next morning, dressing in his fine new clothes and impatient to leave. Mamá and Luís were breakfasting on beans and *tortillas*. Ramon was hungry, too, but knew he must not eat food now. This was called "fasting", and it kept the spirit pure. He would be permitted to eat after the ceremony.

Soon enough, they were making their way along Chihuahua's dusty streets toward the cathedral. First Communion took place during the Feast of the Sacred Heart of Jesus every summer, and was a holy day almost as special as Easter. Mamá was wearing her best Sunday dress and a well-worn *mantilla* with which to cover her face when she entered the cathedral.

Ramon left them to go and join the other boys assembling in the chapel. Some girls were there as well, wearing white dresses with veils, and flowers in their hair. They were giggling, but Ramon and his friends stood somewhat apart, trying to look dignified.

The deacon came then, to arrange the boys into a line, and a nun did likewise for the girls. There came a great burst of music from inside and then the sounds of singing. With their hands folded prayerfully at their breasts, the children left the chapel and began their stately procession into the cathedral.

They marched up the center aisle, while the people seated in the pews sang and turned to watch them go by. At the altar the children halted, for there was the bishop waiting for them, dressed all in white and gold, with a tall miter on his head and holding the jeweled shepherd's crook that symbolized his position as leader of the flock.

The bishop blessed the children and they sat, looking about at the white *yucca* flowers decorating the altar and trying hard not to fidget through the long Mass. Ramon sang the Latin responses along with the rest of the children and before he knew it, the moment had come. He and the others lined up before the bishop and, one by one, received their First Holy Communion.

"This is the Body of Christ," intoned the bishop as he placed the bit of blessed bread onto Ramon's tongue.

"Amen," responded Ramon, and he was filled with joy. He could now receive Holy Communion any time he attended Mass, and the King of

Heaven would reside in his heart for the rest of his days.

The Mass drew to a close and the choir led the congregation in a glorious swell of song as the children proceeded down the aisle and on outside. From there they were guided toward the nearby school where another surprise awaited Ramon.

A breakfast had been prepared for the children who, hungry from their night of fasting, grew wide-eyed as they beheld the feast. Mangoes, melons, grapes, and oranges had been laid out in colorful array, and platters were heaped with lamb and pork meat. Someone had made small fruit pies called *empanadas*, and there was sweet *pan de leche* and even a custard *flan*, with cold milk to wash it all down.

Ramon ate until he was stuffed, wondering if he might be able to sneak some of the treats home for his family to share. But soon there was nothing left except for empty plates and burping children.

It had been a wonderful, exciting morning, and now everyone was eager to be away home. Ramon and his friends said goodbye as they left the school.

When Ramon reached his house, he found Mamá waiting there for him in the doorway. She stood there silently, and he wondered why she hadn't yet spoken.

Then he remembered from catechism class that he was now expected to kiss her hand in the ritual greeting of a First Communicant to his *mamá*. He did so, and when he looked up Mamá's eyes were shining. She smiled at him then, and gathered him into her arms and hugged him hard. Ramon's heart swelled with pride.

Chapter 6

SWEET SPRINGTIME

"AND here is one for you, Ramon."

The soft, buttery *cajeta* candy stuck to Ramon's teeth as he popped it into his mouth and chewed. "Thank you, Tía."

His *tía* Lupe smiled and ruffled his hair. "Mind you and Josefita don't eat the whole box," she warned good-naturedly as the two children headed for the door.

"We won't, Mamá." Josefita waved cheerfully.

Ramon waved, too, fully aware of his responsibility. Now that he and his cousin were older, they were expected to help earn money, and so every day after school Ramon would come to his *tía's* house to fetch the sweets she had made for them to sell. Josefita was no longer in school, staying home instead to help with chores so her mother was free to make the candies.

The spring winds made the air feel warm after the cold dryness of another desert winter, and Ramon and Josefita wandered contentedly along the Alameda, calling to passersby to come buy their wares. Many people were out enjoying the day, sitting about on benches, or riding bicycles.

"I've never ridden a bicycle, have you?" asked Ramon.

Josefita chuckled and shook her head. Who would teach a *girl* to ride a bicycle?

"If I had a bicycle," continued Ramon, "I'd ride it every day. I'd ride it all day long and never get tired. I'd ride it clear to America!"

Josefita laughed, and Ramon scowled.

"Why are you laughing at me?" he demanded.

"No, not you," chuckled Josefita. "What you just said. It reminded me of a funny story my friend Modesta told me once, back in school."

"What was it?"

"Well, there was this boy, he lived up north in Juarez, near the border of America. Every day he would ride his bicycle across the bridge into El Paso, Texas."

Ramon grinned. Lucky boy!

"And every day," continued Josefita, "the customs officials would stop him and search him to see if he was smuggling anything."

Ramon stopped grinning. He knew smuggling was a very serious crime. Anyone caught trying to carry jewelry, or clothing, or even food into the United States to sell would be severely punished. Even the sweets he and his cousin were peddling were worth far more in the U.S. than in Mexico, and many people thought the extra money was worth the risk.

"Did they ever find anything?" asked Ramon.

"Well, no, not really. They looked in his pockets, and in his shoes, anywhere they thought he might be hiding something. They never found anything, and so would always send him along on his way. Every day they would search him, and every day they let him ride his bicycle on into the U.S."

"So what finally happened?" Ramon was eager to hear how the story ended.

Josefita swatted idly at a bee before continuing.

"Somebody finally figured out that it was *bicycles* he was smuggling across the border!"

Ramon laughed and Josefita laughed with him. It had been a good day, full of sunshine and breezes and even an occasional tiny hummingbird coming to buzz about their heads before flitting off along the Alameda. The children had sold most of their wares and were now sprawled idly on the ground.

"What are you learning now in school?" wondered Josefita after a while.

"Geography, and literature. And catechism, of course." Ramon tried not to think of Don Jimenez and his bricks.

"Tell me something," his cousin begged him. "I miss school. Tell me something about literature."

Ramon thought hard, trying to remember his last lesson.

" '*Pobre barquilla mia, entre penascos rota. . .*' " *My poor little boat, there among the rocks. . .* He recited the great Lope de Vega's poem of a boat sailing through the hardships of life. With his eyes drowsily closed, he was so caught up in the poem's beauty that he scarcely even noticed the fading daylight until Josefita sighed.

"We should be going home now," she said.

"Not yet. Let's stay just a bit longer." Although people were beginning to leave the Alameda, Ramon hoped he and his cousin could sell all of the sweets they had brought. Mamá and Tía would split the money, and Mamá had told Ramon that she was saving the money for something very special.

"I want for you to go to the university when you are older," she had told him not long ago.

Ramon was very excited by this. "You think I can go to the university?" It would be a great honor to grow up to become a scholar.

"*Sí, mi hijo.* You are very smart, very good with your head. You could learn much in a university and make something of yourself."

"It would cost many, many *pesos.*" But with an education he could become employed, earn enough money to move to America with Mamá and Luís.

Ramon never lost sight of this goal. He studied hard in school, and worked tirelessly to sell his wares.

"Come on," he said, helping Josefita to her feet. "There's not much left." Josefita's basket of sweets was nearly empty, and Ramon was down to his last few pieces of *cajeta* candy. "Let's finish up and then go home."

THE following Sunday was very windy, with no one on the Alameda, and so Mamá took Ramon and Luís to visit with their other *tía*, Lola. Ramon and Luís always enjoyed visiting her, for her son Isidro, unlike themselves, had a great many toys to play with.

"I don't want Ramon and Luís to receive toys for their birthdays," Mamá would say to people. "I much prefer that you give them clothes."

Someday when I have children I will give them clothes, and toys, too, Ramon secretly promised himself, enchanted by Isidro's small kaleidoscope. When held to the light and turned, bits of colored glass tumbled about to form bright stars. Beside him, Luís was shaking a glass globe filled with water and watching snow swirl about inside it.

From the kitchen he could hear Mamá's voice and Tía Lola's as they mixed *tamale* dough. Once he even heard Mamá laugh. It was good to hear her laugh. Ramon found himself wishing, yet again, that they didn't have to be so poor, that Mamá wouldn't have to work so hard and could have more time to spend enjoying herself.

Luís, too, was tired of constantly having to do without.

"If I helped Ramon and Josefita to sell things," he asked Mamá later that day as they were walking home, "would we have enough money to buy toys like Isidro's?"

They were just then passing the bakery, and the smell of bread filled the air.

"You should be careful walking in front of the bakery," answered Mamá, clutching Luís's small hand in her own, "because they take children who ask for toys and throw them into the oven!"

Ramon looked at her, horrified, and saw that she was only joking. Luís giggled and hugged her, saying he loved her and promising to ask for no more toys.

"That is good," said Mamá, "because we must save our money carefully."

The wind had died by now and it was quite pleasant out. When they reached home, Ramon set a chair outside for Mamá to sit and prepare the *tamales*. Earlier that morning he had placed some dried corn husks in a bowl of water to soak, and now he and Mamá would fill them with the dough she and Tía Lola had made and then steam them.

Going back inside for the soaking husks, he took them out of the water and was patting them dry with a rag when he heard a knock at the door.

"Here, Luís," he said, handing his brother the damp bundle. "Take these to Mamá while I see who it is."

The sun shining through the front window made a great square of warm yellow light on the earthen floor as Ramon crossed the room and opened the door. A man stood there, likely someone from one of the nearby villages by the look of the *burro*-cart waiting in the road.

"*Sí?*" Ramon inquired politely.

"Is this where Anastacia Ortiz lives?" The man looked uncomfortable, holding his *sombrero* in his hands and looking down at the floor. "I have a message for her. She must come to Meoqui."

"What is it? What is the matter?" Mamá had come to the door and stood beside Ramon. She placed a hand on Ramon's shoulder and waited for the man's reply.

"It is your *mamá*," the man said to her. "She is very sick, *señora*. The *padre* says she is going to die. You must come home to Meoqui at once."

Chapter 7

LIFE WITH TÍO PABLO

RAMON, standing between Mamá and Luís, pushed up another prayer bead on his rosary. “Hail, Mary, full of grace. . .” Tío Pablo and the other men shoveled rocky yellow dirt over the grave, while everyone around them prayed.

Mamá’s face was hidden behind her black *mantilla*, but Ramon knew she was weeping. He had never seen her cry, not even after Papá had died.

At least we arrived in time for her to say goodbye, he thought, remembering their hasty departure yesterday and the trip here in the dark in that man’s *burro*-cart. Mamá’s *mamá*, Ramon’s *abuelita*, had opened her eyes when Mamá knelt at the bed, and smiled when Mamá took her hand. They had prayed together all night, and by dawn she had passed peacefully away.

Ramon yawned. He and Luís had prayed, too, for as long as they could stay awake. Then they had curled up on the floor and fallen asleep, to be awakened later in the morning for the funeral.

Beside him, Luís fidgeted. Too little sleep, and now too long on his feet in the hot sun. But the *padre* was intoning the final benediction, with the mourners chanting the solemn response and bowing their heads before turning to leave.

Mamá silently took Ramon and Luís by the hand. They followed Tío Pablo as he led them away from the graveyard and back to his tiny *casa*.

Ramon knew something was different now, but it was not until later that day as he watched the way Tío Pablo treated Mamá that he began to realize what it was.

"My brother Pablo is not very smart," Mamá explained gently as she cleaned up the meal Tío Pablo had just finished. Ramon's belly growled, and he wondered when he and Luís could eat.

"No woman ever married him," Mamá continued, "and so my *mamá* took care of him. But now she is gone." Mamá's eyes filled with tears, and Ramon impulsively reached out and took her hand. "She is gone, and I must care for him, and you and Luís must both be very strong now."

"I am strong, Mamá. I am growing fast!"

"*Sí, mi hijo.*" Tears spilled down Mamá's cheeks, and she smiled and hugged Ramon hard. "You are my big, strong son. But it is a different kind of strength you will need now, the strength Jesus had when people spat and threw stones at him."

Ramon began to feel uneasy. "How long will we stay here?"

"I do not know," replied Mamá. "A long time perhaps."

"But. . .when will we be returning home?"

Mamá's response was so quiet that Ramon almost didn't hear it.

"This is our home now."

This is our home now.

More and more over the next weeks, Ramon came to realize how those few simple words had changed everything. Mamá was no longer head of the *casa* as she had been back in Chihuahua. This was Tío Pablo's *casa*.

Mamá's *papá* had died long ago, and so her brother Pablo had always been in charge. In Mexico, men ruled the home, and a woman had to do as she was told. Women had to walk behind the men, eat when the men had finished, and not speak unless they were spoken to.

Back in Chihuahua Ramon had never noticed this, because Mamá had lived on her own without Papá. More importantly, Chihuahua was a large and modern place where visitors brought new ideas and showed people different ways to think and to live. Only sometimes would Ramon see a woman stop talking as her husband approached, or walk behind him on her way to Mass.

But Meoqui was a small village, and the people lived here as they always had, according to the old ways. The women did not speak much at all, certainly not if there were men around. In fact, they scarcely even left their homes. They were furtive when they ventured out on errands, as though they feared to be away from their *casas* for too long.

Ramon missed the gaiety of the city, the bright colors of the ladies's dresses and even the men's white clothes. Meoqui was a poor community and everybody here just wore dirty brown. He missed the shops and the bustle, and the bicycles on the Alameda, Mass in the great cathedral on Sundays.

He tried to be strong, as Mamá had bid him. At first he had thought that being poor here would not be much different than being poor in Chihuahua. Here everybody was poor.

But it was living with Tío Pablo that made them so miserable.

"He hit Mamá again last night," said Luís one day, tugging his wide *sombrero* a bit lower to shade his face. He and Ramon were weeding the beanfield behind Tío Pablo's shabby *casa* as they did every day, stooping for endless hours in the scorching sun.

"What did he say she'd done this time?"

"Said she'd burnt his beans again."

Ramon grunted in disgust. Mamá was a fine cook and never burned anything. Tío Pablo simply liked hitting people, especially women. He said it kept them in their proper place.

"Did he get a job today?" he asked his brother.

"*Sí*, Señor Lopez needed men to help make bricks." Luís's nimble fingers dug in the soil to pluck out the sprouting weeds. "He might even ask him back again tomorrow."

Ramon supposed this was good. He could never make up his mind if he preferred days his *tío* was present or days when he was not. When he was home he beat and shouted at the boys all day long. When he was absent the boys were left alone to work in peace, but it would be worse in the evening when Tío Pablo stormed back into the *casa*, cursing, sometimes drunk, and always ready to strike at whoever was closest.

That evening was no different. The hungry boys sat at the table, waiting for their *tío's* return so they could eat. It was late when he finally arrived, stomping inside and slamming the door.

Tío Pablo pulled the sweaty shirt over his head and tossed it onto the dirt floor before falling into a chair and pounding the table with his fists.

"Where is my water? Bring me my water so I can wash!"

Mamá bent to pick up the soiled shirt, then hurried to the stove to pour hot water from a kettle into the wash basin as fast as she could, scrambling to carry it to the table without spilling any.

Ramon and Luís were holding their breaths, hoping he would not strike her.

"What are you looking at?" Too late, the boys realized he was addressing them. A sudden backhanded blow sent Luís sprawling from his chair onto the floor. Mamá clenched her eyes shut, and Ramon could see her lips move ever so slightly in prayer. *As we forgive those who trespass against us.*

Luís rose unsteadily to his feet and limped to the door. Ramon followed.

"You boys better not come back here until that beanfield is weeded! That's right, I saw it. You've done nothing all day. Nothing! A couple of lazy *mocosos*, that's what you are."

Ramon did not wait to hear more. He and Luís went outside to sit in the dirt and watch the sun go down as they waited for their *tío* to eat. Ramon pretended not to notice Luís's sniffling, but he heard his brother's words clearly.

"I want to go home."

The next day he and Luís had scarcely started their weeding when they heard Tío Pablo come storming angrily back from town.

I guess Señor Lopez didn't need his help today, after all. Ramon concentrated very hard on the tiny weed he was pulling, careful not to look up lest he attract his *tío's* attention. But it didn't matter, for before long the man was striding toward them in the beanfield, carrying his whip.

"You should have finished this entire field by now you lazy—" Finishing his sentence with words Ramon did not know, Tío Pablo raised the whip and laid into the unfortunate boy. The ends stung Ramon's skin and ripped his shirt, which Mamá would now have to mend.

Ramon gritted his teeth and took one deep breath after another, trying to ignore the pain. Soon Tío Pablo had tired of lashing him and swaggered away to the *casa*, no doubt to slap at Mamá before taking a bottle of *tequila* with him to bed. The boys continued their work in silence until time to go in for the noon meal.

The smell of frying *enchiladas* greeted them as they entered the *casa*, but Mamá hastily set this food aside.

"No, no, you must not eat those. They are for your *tío*."

Luís scowled, watching as Mamá reached for the stack of moldy *tortillas* that Tío Pablo permitted them to eat. Mamá took a *tortilla* and tore it in half, giving one piece to each boy. Ramon accepted his without a word and went to curl up in the corner where a hard straw mattress served as a bed for all three of them.

Mamá returned to the hearth, where a pot of laundry gently bubbled. In addition to her own washing, some people in the village paid her to do theirs as well. Sometimes, since nobody here had much schooling, they even paid her to write letters for them, or to read letters they had received. Of course, Tío Pablo made her give the money to him.

Ramon rubbed at the welt left by the whipping, then wished he hadn't, for Mamá noticed him and came over to see it.

"I know it is hard, *mi hijo*. But we can be strong." She passed him a small crock of lard for rubbing into the sore skin, then plucked a needle from her pocket and helped him remove the ripped shirt. A few deft stitches neatly mended the tear. She placed the shirt over Ramon's head and tugged, then abruptly stopped.

"What is this?" she asked, pushing aside Ramon's tousled black hair for a better look at the rash on his neck.

"I don't know," he answered, coughing slightly. "It just appeared a few days ago." He raised a sleeve to blot at his runny nose.

Mamá said no more as she watched him finish pulling on his shirt. She appeared to be thinking very hard about something.

By that night the rash on Ramon's neck had spread to his chest, and Mamá found a similar rash beginning on Luís. The following morning she made a special trip to the market and returned with a sack of limes.

"I will tell your *tío* that you are not to work in the field tomorrow, either of you," she told the boys as she felt their foreheads.

"He will be very angry," Luís pointed out.

Mamá snorted. "Unless I am mistaken, he will soon be too sick himself to care. Now here, drink this lime juice and go lie down." Luís dutifully did so, with Ramon following him. It was the last thing Ramon remembered clearly.

Chapter 8

WHY IS LIFE SO HARD?

WHEN Ramon awoke again, something seemed different. He sat up on the straw mattress, trying to determine what had changed. His head began to ache terribly and he was forced to lie back down.

What is it? he wondered as he lay there, listening to the sounds around him. Gradually it came to him that the difference was those very sounds. Snuffling sounds. Moans. The crying of a baby.

A baby? In Tío Pablo's *casa*?

Ignoring the pain in his head, Ramon sat up again.

The *casa* was dark, although it seemed to be day outside. Someone had tacked a large rag across the window.

Looking about, Ramon saw people all around him, lying on the dirt floor. The table had been pushed up against the adobe wall to make room for more. He smelled vinegar, and noticed for the first time the damp cloth on his forehead.

Mamá! Where was Mamá? He stifled his sudden fright and looked about, quickly spotting her where she knelt over one of the stricken people as she held something to the man's lips. Lime juice. Ramon remembered the lime juice he had drunk, and realized he had been sick, that all these people must be sick.

He wondered where Luís was, and a moment later saw his brother hurrying toward him.

"Ramon! It is good to see you awake at last." Luís flopped down beside him.

"I have been ill?"

"*Sí*. I was, too, but Mamá said I didn't get it so bad because she treated it in time. She saw that you were coming down with the measles and knew she must prepare. Good thing, too," Luís added, with a nod at the people lying about the room.

"It looks like half the village is here," observed Ramon. "She must be very busy."

"I help her," said Luís, with pride in his voice. "I squeeze the limes for people to drink, and I keep rags soaking in vinegar to cool the skin. Oh, look, here she comes."

"*Mi hijo*!" Ramon heard Mamá say as she picked her way across the crowded room toward him. "You are feeling better?" She gently pushed back his sweaty hair and felt his forehead, then bent to give him a hug.

He told her that he was feeling weak, and she sent Luís for a bowl of rice. Then he slept again, and by evening he felt strong enough to begin helping Luís soak the rags. A few more sick people arrived, but Mamá said that many people were getting well now, and would soon be returning to their homes.

Tío Pablo could be heard from time to time yelling to Mamá from his bed. Mamá would bring him rice mixed with bits of chicken meat, and tasty *menudo* soup made with pork and tripe. Ramon tried to feel sorry that Tío Pablo had been sick, but mostly he was just glad his *tío* was too weak to hit Mamá.

Soon, however, everyone was well again, even Tío Pablo. Mamá spent a few afternoons visiting those who had been ill to see if she could provide any further aid to them, but a black eye quickly let her know how Tío Pablo felt about that.

She resumed her laundry work and letter writing, and also began making candy from the tender *nopales* of the prickly pear cactus to sell as Tía Lupe had done, even getting Tío Pablo's grudging permission to allow the boys to skip weeding on Sundays so they could peddle it about the village. Ramon gave the money to Mamá, who quietly gave some back to him with the advice that he hide it from his *tío*.

Ramon would bury his share of the money beneath a large cactus, Mamá would give the rest of the money to Tío Pablo, and Tío Pablo would beat them all for being lazy slackers. Life went on.

"Just remember," Mamá said one day as she mended their ripped clothing and bruised flesh, "that Jesus suffered, too, so that we could have salvation."

The suffering of Jesus Christ was very much on everyone's minds during the weeks of Lent that led up to Easter Sunday. For forty days there was fasting, and prayer, and penance of every kind as the people prepared to celebrate the death and resurrection of their Savior.

A crown of thorns, such as the one Jesus had been forced to wear, was placed on the door of the small church where Ramon now served as an altar boy. Tomorrow was Holy Thursday, and he would be assisting the *padre* at Mass.

Tonight he was preparing the church, scrubbing the floors and the windows and making sure the beeswax candles were in place. Mamá had already washed all the linens, and Ramon now carefully laid them out. The last thing he did before leaving was fill a basin with water and set out a snowy white towel beside it on the altar, to be used in the foot-washing ceremony.

The following afternoon, as the villagers were shuffling into the church, Ramon approached an old man.

"*Señor*," he asked formally, as instructed, "will you participate in the *lavoratorio*, the foot-washing?"

Greatly honored, the old man agreed, and followed Ramon to a small alcove where Ramon then scrubbed the man's feet in preparation for the ceremony. Giving the man a pair of white linen slippers to wear, Ramon escorted him to the front of the church to await the ceremony.

The Mass began. Padre Gutierrez led the *Kyrie* and read the Gospel.

" '*Lord, you shall never wash my feet!*' " Ramon heard the familiar words of the apostle Peter, who was surprised that Jesus Christ would wish to do something so lowly.

" '*Behold.*' " Now it was Jesus who spoke. " '*If I wash your feet, so you must also go and do.*' "

It was time for the ceremony to begin. Ramon led the man to the altar and bade him sit down. Removing the linen slippers, Padre Gutierrez dipped a cloth into the basin and gently bathed the feet, drying them with the towel. The lesson implied in the words of the wise Jesus was clear: Follow my example. I am not too important to care for others.

Ramon was reminded of Mamá caring for the sick people after the measles outbreak. Jesus must be very proud of Mamá. Ramon hoped he could live a life like that, too.

Then he remembered the black eyes, the way Tío Pablo yelled at her and gave her skimpy portions of food to eat. He thought of the whippings he and Luís endured in the beanfield, how hungry they were all the time.

Why is there so much suffering? he wondered. *I know, Lord Jesus, that you suffered when people beat you, tortured you, even killed you. But why does life have to be like that?*

The following day was even sadder, for this was Good Friday, the day when the villagers solemnly remembered the death of Jesus.

The altar was now completely bare, covered by only a white cloth and with a large cross hanging high above it. Jesus had been nailed by the Romans to such a cross, and had hung from it for three hours before dying.

Bowed from the whipping he had received, bleeding from the crown of thorns on his head, Jesus had carried the heavy cross through the streets of Nazareth as people jeered and threw stones at him. Then he had looked down from the cross at the people who had done this to him.

" *'Father, forgive them, for they know not what they do.'* "

Ramon pondered this. Was he supposed to forgive Tío Pablo for the way he treated Ramon's family? Could he? He thought of the endless days sweating in the beanfield, of Mamá cooking *tamales* and *enchiladas* for Tío Pablo while she was given only moldy *tortillas* to eat.

Gazing up at the cross, Ramon wondered again, *Why does life have to be filled with suffering?*

Chapter 9

A NEW JOB

WELL, at least I'm out of the beanfield now.

It was a lovely summer afternoon, and Ramon paused for a moment in his labors to breathe in the scent of blooming *yuccas* and smile at the hummingbirds that flitted about. Having finished his altar boy chores for the morning, he was now engaged in one of the additional tasks to which he had recently been promoted: helping with Padre Gutierrez's household responsibilities.

Sundays, and every weekday after school, Ramon could now be found working at either the church or the *padre's* home. Tío Pablo had not been pleased to lose Ramon's free labor, but even he must abide by the wishes of the *padre*, who had taken a liking to Ramon. Now, if only Luís could come work here, too. . .

"Hey, Ramon, how about a little help here?" Startled, Ramon realized he was falling behind in his task. His friend, Juan, was hoisting baskets of *tortillas* into a small handcart. Ramon was supposed to be filling the baskets, but when he looked up it was to see his impatient friend filling them by himself.

Ramon grinned sheepishly. “Sorry,” he apologized, grabbing up more *tortillas* and adding them to the basket. “I guess my mind was wandering.”

Juan returned the grin, replying, “On a beautiful day like this, who can blame you?” The big, strapping boy loaded the basket onto the cart. “But still, let’s hurry. I want to meet up with some friends of mine this evening after we’re done here.”

All this food—stacks of *tortillas*, loaves of bread, cheese, butter, jugs of milk, and sometimes even *tamales*, *empanadas*, or *menudo* soup—was left for the *padre* every Sunday by villagers attending the Mass. Ramon and Juan were to gather up everything and wheel it around to the *padre’s* home, as they were doing now.

As they approached the small *casa*, Ramon waved to Mamá, who was just now, along with one or two other villagers, riding away in the church’s horse-cart. She, too, now worked for the *padre*. Not only did she clean the church as she had back in Chihuahua, but she also assisted in collecting the *primísias*, tributes similar to the foodstuffs gathered by the boys but consisting primarily of livestock or produce to keep the *padre* well fed.

Ramon knew that when Mamá returned, the cart would be filled with baskets of mangoes, limes, and corn, and also with chickens, pigs, and maybe even a goat.

Mamá was paid by the *padre* for her work. Ramon, although his services as altar boy and household assistant were unpaid, would be given some of the food that he was now delivering, and which he would share with Mamá and Luís when Tío Pablo wasn't looking. With Luís continuing to sell candy and hide some of the money, the small family was now living almost as well as they had in Chihuahua.

A poke in the arm reminded him that he was woolgathering again and that there was still work to be done.

"It's just that the circus is in town, and my friends and I want to go see it later when I'm finished with my chores here," explained Juan.

Ramon knew about the circus. All week he'd heard his friends talking of how it would be stopping to give a small show in Meoqui on its way to perform in Chihuahua.

"You have money to go see the circus?" Ramon was astonished. He wasn't sure exactly what a circus was, but he knew it had many exciting things to see. And also that it cost money to visit.

"Well, no," said Juan as he and Ramon unloaded the food from the cart into Padre Gutierrez's kitchen. "Not exactly. But since it will be stopping here for the night, we plan to sneak into it. Say," he added, dropping his voice to a whisper and looking about to make sure no one was listening. "You want to join us?"

"Oh, no. I don't think so." Go roaming about in the dark of night? Sneak into a circus? Ramon knew what Mamá would have to say about that!

"Oh, well, it was just a thought," said Juan. "Let me know if you change your mind."

Together they wheeled the empty cart to its shed and returned to the *padre's casa* to complete the remainder of the afternoon's chores. Ramon always enjoyed this part of the day, because the work was done on the *patio*.

Padre Gutierrez's *patio* was a magnificent affair, red brick and colorful tile, with flowers along every wall and in every corner and even twining overhead to provide shade, and with a well in the center. It never got too hot, and the air was filled with the perfume of the flowers.

But what made it so spectacular was the aviary filled with exotic birds. Parrots and macaws and cockatoos and all manner of brightly-plumed species fluttered and squawked in their great enclosure. Ramon often took home small feathers of green or blue for Luís to play with.

He looked about for some now as he swung open the door and entered, pocketing a few of the more attractive feathers that had drifted into the corner of the great cage. Then, moving very slowly so as not to frighten the birds, he began to sweep out the floor while his friend bent to scrub it.

"I saw a *peso* in the collection basket at Mass this morning," he remarked to Juan. The poor local people rarely had anything more than an occasional *centavo* to contribute to the church. "Probably from Señor Oaxaca," he added, referring to the richest man in town.

Juan nodded. "I hear he bought a silver mine recently." No doubt there would be cash money circulating around Meoqui for the next few weeks as the wealthy gentleman made various purchases. This was good news for the villagers.

Just then the birds in the aviary began to cry out and flap wildly into the air. Looking up, Ramon saw Padre Gutierrez stooping to brush past the red roses that twined up the *patio's* entrance arch. Pausing a moment to inhale their fragrance, he continued over the tiled *patio* to where the boys were working in the aviary.

With a nod to the boys, the *padre* swung open the aviary door and stepped inside.

"Hello Antonio, hello Francis, and where is. . .ah, there's my Theresa." He smiled as the birds flew down from their perches to settle on his arm as others flew about his head in joyous greeting.

Ramon leaned against his broom and gazed at the sight that never failed to amaze him: the *padre* with his gentle, beautiful birds. As he watched, Theresa, a small blue parakeet, alighted on the man's finger and reached forward with her hooked beak to nip him fondly on the nose. Ramon laughed with delight, and the startled birds flapped away back to their wooden perches.

Slapping his dusty hands briskly against his trousers, the *padre* turned to address Ramon.

"I've been summoned to Santa Eulalia and will not return from there until tomorrow." He reached into a pocket and pulled out a large key on a cord, which he handed to Ramon. "Please be so good as to lock up the church tonight and unlock it again in the morning."

Solemnly, Ramon accepted the key, looping it over his head so that it hung down in front. "*Sí, padre*," he said, his eyes wide. Being left in charge of the church was a big responsibility!

"What a lucky break," said Juan once the *padre* had left the *patio*. "With him gone for the rest of the day, I can quit early to go meet my friends. Are you sure you don't want to come with us?"

Swinging the aviary door shut behind him, Ramon went to the well to draw some water for the flowers.

"I—I don't know, Juan." Ramon was torn. A chance to go see the circus! An opportunity like this might never come again.

But Juan was older, a teenager, and some of his chums were known to cause trouble on occasion. Ramon was not at all sure he wished to accompany them on a risky outing such as this.

"Oh, don't worry," said Juan as he helped Ramon with the watering. "We'll wait till after dark so we won't get caught. And we'll be back with plenty of time for you to unlock the church," he hastily added, seeing Ramon's dubious look.

"Well, as long as we're back by dawn I guess it will be all right." Ramon knew Mamá would worry. But he was no longer a child, and perhaps this was a good way to let her know that he needn't ask her permission for everything he did.

Juan grinned and slapped him on the back. "It'll be great fun. You'll see."

Ramon grinned back at him. What an adventure! He could hardly wait.

Chapter 10

OFF TO THE CIRCUS

"YOU go first!"

"No, I don't want to get caught. You go!"

"You won't get caught if you're quiet, *idiota*!" scoffed a third. Soon the entire group was shoving at each other, until Ramon was certain a fight would break out. Nervously, he began to edge away.

"Hey, let's send *him*!"

In the moment of silence that followed, Ramon had a sudden sinking feeling, and looked up to see everyone staring at him.

"Yeah, he's little. Nobody'll notice him."

Ramon shot a quick, helpless look to Juan, who returned a sheepish grin and a shrug. *What's to worry about*, he seemed to say. *It's just a lark.*

Just a lark. Ramon snorted, wondering how he had gotten into this mess. *I could be home now, eating beans and rice with Mamá and Luís, instead of crouching behind a clump of cactus in the dark with a bunch of rowdy boys.* Some fun this had turned out to be.

But gradually he began to warm to the spirit of the adventure. The older boys had elected *him* to scout ahead and make sure nobody was guarding the place. He could do this!

That afternoon, he and Juan had hastily quit their chores and, after first pausing to pocket a few *tortillas* from Padre Gutierrez's kitchen, had walked to a warehouse by the train tracks outside town to meet up with Juan's teenaged friends. There, Ramon had watched uneasily as they'd whiled away the next few hours drinking and playing at various games.

Toward dusk, as the shadows of *agaves* and *ocotillos* crept across the hard, stony sand, they'd put away their cards and dice and ambled off down the railroad track, arriving at the great circus tent just as the sun went down. Once there, they'd scuttled behind the scant cover of a nearby prickly pear cactus and watched as the circus personnel secured the area for the night.

As it grew later, the boys had become more impatient. One had pulled tobacco from his pocket and rolled it into a cigarette, but scarcely had he lit it when it was snatched from his lips by his companions. "Fool!" they cried, stamping it into the sand until it was completely extinguished. "It will be smelled by the guards, if they have not already seen you light it."

"What guards?" replied the indignant smoker. "I see none. They have all left."

There had followed a heated argument regarding exactly *where* the men had gone, with nervous glances toward the boxcars along the track. Hence their need for someone to scout ahead, and Ramon's current predicament.

Knowing that the boys were depending on him gave him a sense of pride, as well as the courage to proceed. Crouching low in the moonlight, he shuffled quickly over the sand from cactus to cactus, hoping he would not step on a rattlesnake, and gradually he drew close to the tent.

It was larger than any tent he had ever seen, larger even than the village church.

I think it might even be bigger than the cathedral in Chihuahua! Creeping swiftly around to the rear, with constant furtive glances to be sure he was not seen, Ramon gingerly lifted the canvas bottom of the tent an inch or so above the ground. His heart was pounding as he peered underneath.

Nothing. No alarm was sounded, no guards appeared to drag him away. He'd done it!

Lifting the canvas a little higher, he poked his head inside. It was too dark to see anything, but he had the impression of vastness filled with towering piles of shadowy shapes. Turning to the moonlit desert behind him, he signaled the boys.

"There's nobody here! Come on over," he called in a loud whisper.

Needing no further encouragement, they swarmed eagerly from their hiding place and scrambled under the tent.

"Well done, Ramon! Good job!" they congratulated him.

Ramon puffed out his chest and beamed with pride. "I wasn't scared at all," he said.

Everybody laughed, and Juan slapped him on the back.

"Hey, it's dark in here," someone noted. "Anybody got a light?"

The boy who had earlier tried to smoke a cigarette produced matches, and within moments they had located and lit a kerosene lantern.

"Only one," somebody else cautioned, nodding in the direction of the boxcars, "or they might notice it."

Even by the light of just one lantern there was much to see. The boys quickly split up and began prowling about the place, opening crates and pulling away tarps. Fascinating discoveries were made, and puzzling ones, too.

"Hey, what's this?" said a boy. A small can of something resembling whitewash was held up for inspection.

"I think that's for painting on the face." Further rummaging produced a red rubber ball and a wig, and in no time at all the boy had gleefully made himself up as a silly-looking clown.

"Look what I've found," said another triumphantly. They turned to see that he was wearing a black top hat and a cape. "I'm the ringmaster!"

"And now you think you can order us around?" somebody snickered, and all the boys laughed.

Ramon was having a high old time, laughing gaily with his new friends as he explored the various trappings and props of the big tent. In one corner he discovered a rack from which hung many sequined costumes for beautiful women to wear. Selecting one, a sleek, shiny item resembling a swimsuit, he held it up so the sequins sparkled in the light of the lamp.

"*Mira*, look what Ramon's got!"

"*Sí*, Ramon, try it on for us, why don't you?"

With flaming face, Ramon hastily replaced the costume on the rack.

A sound from above caught everyone's attention and the boys looked up to see one of their companions climbing a ladder to where a trapeze had been secured.

"*Ay*, come down from there before you get yourself killed, *muchacho!*" they called to him.

Ignoring their entreaties, the daring youth reached the top of the ladder and untied the trapeze. Ramon held his breath, wondering what would happen next. Did the boy really mean to swing high over their heads on the dangerous-looking device?

He did. Grasping the trapeze awkwardly in his hands, the boy uttered a wild yell and leaped from the platform, swinging in a wide arc from one end of the huge tent to the other.

But on the return swing, something went wrong. One hand came loose, and he dangled for a horrible moment even as the trapeze continued its swing. Crying out in sudden terror, he slipped off completely and plummeted through the air, landing, fortunately, in a broad net that had been strung beneath the trapeze.

"*Ay*, Roberto, are you all right?" His friends came rushing to his assistance, with Ramon bringing up the rear.

"Never mind that," another said. "We've got to get out of here. Someone might have heard you."

There were murmurs of assent, and the lamp was hastily extinguished as the boys scrambled back out of the tent. Once outside, they crouched in the moonlight, listening uneasily for any sound of their discovery. Hearing none, they began to grin and congratulate one another on the success of their caper.

"Hey, Ramon," said Juan, coming to join his friend, "did you see the look on Roberto's face as he fell?" The burly youth chortled at the memory of his unfortunate fellow.

A sudden roar split the night, and the gang froze in the midst of their horseplay. The sound was like nothing Ramon had ever heard in his life.

Then one of the boys guffawed. "It's a lion, or maybe a tiger. The animals must be caged over there. Come on, let's go see!" And with a wave of his arm, he led the others, still tittering from their fright, through the desert shadows over to where a cluster of small wagons was gathered to one side.

Ramon followed eagerly. A tiger! He couldn't wait to see it. Wait till he told Luís!

There was, indeed, a tiger, as well as an elephant, a gorilla, a rhinoceros, and other animals

Ramon had seen only in books. He moved from one wagon to the next, staring in wonder.

Although at first worried that the roars and growls of the animals would draw attention, Ramon's companions concluded that the nearby circus personnel must be used to such noises in the night, for no one came to investigate. Keeping a wary eye out, the boys spent the next few hours roaming about at will, until daylight began to show in the eastern sky.

"*Ay, caramba!*" Ramon was dismayed. He'd forgotten that he would have to unlock the church at dawn. What was he going to do?

Chapter 11

MAMÁ IS SICK

"WE'VE got to leave, right now," he urged Juan. "We can make it back by dawn if we hurry."

Juan began to press his companions to leave. But to the nervously pacing Ramon it seemed that they took forever to join him. Only the threat of discovery as dawn approached convinced the remaining boys that it was time to leave.

Striding urgently along the dark train tracks, Ramon hoped fervently that he would beat Padre Gutierrez to the church. The horizon began to grow pink, and as they entered town Ramon broke away from the boys. With a wave and a hasty farewell to them, he began a final desperate sprint toward the church.

But his hopes of returning unnoticed were dashed, for standing beside the great wooden door was Padre Gutierrez. His face was like a thundercloud, and when he saw Ramon he grabbed the hapless boy by the ear.

"Where have you been?" he demanded, wrenching the key from Ramon's hand and dragging him along behind as he unlocked the door and strode angrily inside.

"I—" began Ramon, but the *padre* was not listening. Instead, he clouted Ramon smartly on the head and shoved him toward the altar.

"You will kneel there for the entire Mass, and ask Our Lord for forgiveness for your irresponsibility."

Mortified, Ramon knelt on the hard floor while the *padre* went to ring the church bell, as Ramon should have done. Candles were then lit, and linens laid out, all Ramon's chores that he cringed to watch the *padre* perform, and before long people began to enter the church for the morning service.

Fortunately for Ramon, today was not Sunday and many of the villagers were at work, and so the Mass was both shorter and less well attended. It was with great relief that he realized Mamá was away cleaning this morning, and would not have to see his disgrace.

The final prayers were said and the blessing given. When the church was again empty, Padre Gutierrez approached Ramon and sighed loudly.

"Get up and finish your chores," he said, releasing Ramon from his punishment, "and then be off to class." With a disgusted shake of his head he turned and walked away, leaving Ramon to rise stiffly from the floor.

Hobbling about the altar, Ramon gathered the linens and snuffed out the candles. Making quick work of his remaining tasks, he rubbed his knuckles over his bleary eyes and, stifling a yawn, hurried out of the church and over to the school.

Ramon was now in the fourth grade, and doing very well in his studies. He liked school! Except math. Geography was great, literature was even better, but math, well, that was boring. Lately he had taken to writing bits of poetry during math class, and so far had not been caught.

Pushing open the classroom door, Ramon murmured a respectful greeting to the teacher Don Armenta and slipped into his desk. The other pupils began to arrive, and before long the morning's lesson had begun.

By afternoon Ramon could scarcely stay awake. The June sun shone through the window and the buzzing of hummingbirds and bees in the flowers outside merely added to his feeling of drowsiness. In the excitement of his adventure the night before, he had not felt tired, but now the lack of sleep was beginning to catch up with him.

He jerked his nodding head upright in time to see Don Armenta take up a piece of chalk and head for the blackboard. Oh no, the math lesson! Ramon silently groaned as he watched the squeaky chalk write out the figures of the exercise. He wished he could just go to sleep.

Then he had an idea. Leaping to his feet, he clapped his hand over his heart and collapsed dramatically onto the floor, where he lay still.

"Ramon's fainted!" came a cry from one of the other pupils.

"Someone get help!"

"Ramon, are you all right?"

Cracking an eyelid open just the tiniest bit, Ramon saw his fellow classmates leave their desks and come rushing to his side. Even Don Armenta hastily dropped his chalk and hurried over.

"Ramon, can you hear me?" he asked, bending over and slapping briskly at Ramon's face.

That was unpleasant! Ramon decided it was time to "wake up".

"Ohhh," he moaned, fluttering his eyelids and slowly opening his eyes. "What happened?"

"You fainted!" said a classmate, grinning. Such excitement did not normally occur in school.

"Yes, you did faint." Don Armenta helped Ramon to his feet. "Do you think you can walk? You should go and lie down."

Lying down sounded like a great idea to Ramon. Feigning a slight wobbliness, he let his teacher lead him out of the classroom and down the hall to a dark, richly furnished office, where he was told to lie down on a plump velvet sofa. Assuring the *don* that he would be all right, Ramon silently congratulated himself on the success of his ploy and was soon fast asleep.

He was awakened later by someone gently shaking him. Sitting up, he caught sight of a large clock with a swinging brass pendulum, the most magnificent clock he'd ever seen. *Padre Gutierrez must be rich to have clocks and sofas like this in his office.* He remembered the *peso* he'd seen in the collection basket.

The clock showed half past three. School was over now and it was time for him to go do his afternoon church chores. Then he noticed who it was that had awakened him.

"How are you feeling, Ramon?" It was Señor Rivera, the village pharmacist, known for treating illnesses with his various nasty concoctions.

"Much better, thank you." Hopping to his feet to demonstrate his fitness, Ramon began edging toward the door. He dared not be late for chores after the scene this morning, and besides, he was beginning to have an uneasy feeling that his scheme had somehow gone awry.

Sure enough, Señor Rivera produced a small bottle from his pocket and held it out to Ramon.

"Don Armenta sent for me to come give you this. Here, drink it. It will cure the faintness and make you strong."

Hesitantly, Ramon took the bottle and sniffed at the brownish liquid inside. Ugh! He didn't want to drink this. He wasn't even really sick! But Señor Rivera was watching, so Ramon pinched his nose tightly between his fingers and, with a helpless grimace, gulped down the disgusting stuff.

"Here," he said, handing back the empty bottle. "I must go do my chores for the *padre* now."

The pharmacist nodded and replaced the small bottle into his bulging leather bag.

"By the way," he asked, "how is your *mamá* doing? Does she need any more of her medicine?"

Ramon paused, his hand on the heavy iron latch of the door. Mamá was sick?

"What medicine?" he asked, turning back to face Señor Rivera. "What do you mean?"

"Oh, she hasn't told you? I suppose she didn't want to worry you." The man snapped shut his bag and rose to his feet, pausing to pat Ramon reassuringly on the head on his way out the door.

"It's nothing, really," he explained, "just a weakness of the blood following her exposure to the measles. She'll be fine as long as she continues to take my medicine." With that, he strode through the door and away down the corridor, leaving Ramon to make his way to Padre Gutierrez's *patio* with some very puzzled thoughts on his mind.

"Juan, what's a 'weakness of the blood'?" he asked his friend as they pruned the rose bushes.

The older boy shrugged. "Some kind of fever?" he guessed.

Ramon wasn't so sure. Mamá didn't seem sick. Only tired. She always seemed to be tired lately, although this was certainly to be expected with all the work she did caring for Tío Pablo, writing letters for people, cleaning the church, and staying up nights to do people's laundry. Nevertheless, he resolved to watch Mamá closely to see if she was indeed ill.

Over the next weeks, Ramon began to feel some real concern. Mamá wasn't just tired, she seemed exhausted. She had begun to teach Luís to cook the beans and the rice, while she sat at the table with her lips moving in silent prayer. Removing heavy, sopping clothes from the laundry pot required more trips than before as she hoisted them out in smaller batches. Ramon helped her with this task as often as he could.

But what worried him most of all was that of late when Tío Pablo knocked her to the floor, she would lay there for several minutes as if too weak to pull herself to her feet. Even Luís had begun to notice Mamá's condition.

"Mamá is moving a lot more slowly these days, don't you think? Why do you suppose this is? She's not getting old, is she?"

Ramon hushed his younger brother when he talked like this, assuring him that Mamá was just very tired. "She's not old!" he insisted.

But one day as he returned home after his church chores, Mamá met him at the door with a sad and weary look on her face.

"Come here, *mi hijito*. There is something I must tell you." She paused. In the cloudless blue sky above, a lone eagle circled silently. "And something also that I must ask."

His breath catching suddenly in his chest, Ramon felt himself begin to tremble. He didn't think he wanted to hear what came next.

Mamá sighed and wiped her palms slowly on her apron, clearly finding it difficult to continue.

"I am not well," she began, glancing up briefly to meet Ramon's gaze before lowering her eyes once more to the dirt floor. "I've been to see Señor Rivera, who says my blood is weak, and that I must make it strong again. In exchange for cleaning his house he gives me medicine to drink."

She sighed. "But it is not working. I grow weaker. And so now he says I must drink the fresh blood of a cow. This will be very expensive, and I dare not ask your *tío* for the money.

"And so, *mi hijito*," she concluded with a wan smile as she reached out to stroke Ramon's black hair, "I must ask it of you. Will you share with me some of the money you have saved? To go and buy the cow blood?"

Ramon could not believe what he heard. Mamá *was* sick. Very sick! What could he do?

"*Sí*, Mamá," he replied without hesitation. "I will go and buy the blood for you. Tomorrow morning, first thing when the butcher opens. You must not worry," he added, taking her hand in his and squeezing it. "You are going to get better. Someday we will leave this place to go live in America, and I will take care of you!"

He smiled, fighting back the tears. "You will have many dresses to wear, and eat meat every day, and live in a *casa* with a room of your own and big windows."

That night Ramon told Luís of Mamá's illness, and the next morning he went to buy the blood of a freshly-gutted cow. But it did no good, for Mamá drank the blood and became sicker still, developing pneumonia. In fright, Ramon begged Padre Gutierrez to come to the *casa*. The *padre* sat by Mamá's bedside there on the straw mattress in the corner, praying and reading from the Bible long into the night.

Ramon and Luís were dozing at the table when the *padre* came to gently shake them awake.

"Come, you must say goodbye to your *mamá* now. She is calling for you."

Luís's eyes filled with tears, but Ramon clenched his fists and rose stiffly to his feet, determined not to let Mamá see him cry. He knelt by the mattress where Mamá lay too weak to sit up, and held her trembling hand in his while Padre Gutierrez made the sign of the cross on her forehead with holy oil and whispered the prayer of the Last Rites. Luís crept over to lay his head on her breast.

Mamá smiled at her two boys and closed her eyes. One last breath, and then silence. Her life of suffering had ended.

Chapter 12

RAMON ALONE

SHE is with Jesus now.

Ramon kept repeating this to himself as he walked. It was the only thing that kept him going.

His mind was numb as he forced his legs to move, first one and then the other. . . step, then step, then step again. Luís's hand was small and cold in his own.

No more hunger. She was eating heavenly food now. No more beatings. No more hard, weary work. Now she could sing as much as she wanted, with an angel choir. Ramon almost smiled, thinking of this. Yes, Mamá would be happy now.

He and Luís were dressed in black, wearing suits lent to them by Padre Gutierrez, and were winding their way down the street with the rest of the funeral procession. Tío Pablo walked unsteadily in front of them, eyes bloodshot and bleary from a night spent drinking, and before him was Padre Gutierrez leading the procession.

The wagon carrying Mamá was beautifully decorated with flowers and palm fronds, and even the horses had black silk ribbons woven into their harnesses. The villagers, too, were dressed in black as they made their way through the streets of town and out to the cemetery.

Once there, Ramon tried not to look at the fresh hole that had been dug in the ground. Instead he watched as Padre Gutierrez, Tío Pablo, and other men lifted Mamá out of the wagon and laid her into the ground, carefully placing an *adobe* brick beneath her head. Ramon knew the brick represented the suffering of life, and was to add blessings to her soul in heaven.

The *padre* intoned his prayers, and a psalm was sung. Sandy dirt was shoveled over Mamá until the hole was completely filled. All the love Ramon had ever known in his short life was buried at the bottom of that hole. Now the tears he had fought came welling up in his eyes, and he could hold them back no longer. He and Luís clung to each other and cried.

What would become of them now? To stay with Tío Pablo was unthinkable, for he would not take care of them; he only wanted someone to take care of himself.

The answer came a few days later as Padre Gutierrez summoned the boys to his *casa*.

"You have another *tío*, Tío Daniel, whose son is the foreman of Señor Oaxaca's *hacienda* near Chihuahua," he began. "Your Tío Daniel would like for Luís to go and work there on the *hacienda*."

Ramon and Luís looked at each other in astonishment. "Go and work at Señor Oaxaca's *hacienda*?" gasped Ramon. Señor Oaxaca was so rich that his *hacienda* must be a huge and wonderful place. There would always be plenty to eat there.

But wait. "You said our *tío* wants Luís to go there. Not me?"

Without answering, Padre Gutierrez walked slowly over to look out his window.

"You see, Ramon," he explained, "I'd like for you to stay here. You're doing so well in school that it would be a shame to disrupt you. You will live here with me, and continue your schooling and your work here at the church."

"I'd stay here, in Meoqui with you," Ramon repeated, not quite certain he'd heard correctly, "and Luís would go back to Chihuahua to live."

"That's right."

"We'd. . . be separated."

There was a pause before Padre Gutierrez replied.

"Yes."

Ramon was silent for a long moment as the disheartening news sank in. Luís was going to be sent away. He might never see his brother again! After losing Mamá, this was almost more than he could bear. He clenched and unclenched his fists helplessly and tried to breathe.

It wasn't fair! One by one everybody Ramon had ever cared about had been taken away, first Papá, then Mamá, and now Luís.

I'm going to be all alone.

And Luís would be alone, too. Glancing at his brother, Ramon saw how pale and frightened Luís looked.

"I don't want to leave you, Ramon," Luís said in a very small voice.

"It will be all right." *I must be brave for Luís's sake.* Summoning all his willpower, Ramon made himself smile as he clasped Luís's hands in his own. "You're going to go back to Chihuahua! Remember the great cathedral there? And Sunday afternoons on the Alameda? Why, you might even see Josefita again! Of course," he added, "you'll be living outside of town. On a great *hacienda*. I'll bet they have horses there. Wouldn't you like to ride a horse?"

This brought a smile to Luís's face. *He's getting so big,* thought Ramon. His little brother was no longer a baby. Why, only a few months ago Luís had put on Ramon's small white suit and made his own First Holy Communion. Mamá had been so proud of him.

"Mamá would want you to go." This was said with conviction despite Ramon's misgivings. He was not at all sure Mamá would be happy knowing her young sons were to be separated, but surely living on a great *hacienda* would be better than staying with Tío Pablo.

Tío Daniel came the next day to take Luís away, arriving at the church in a sturdy wagon pulled by two horses. Luís had with himself just one small satchel of clothes, which was tossed up into the wagon.

Moments later, Luís was seated in the wagon and waving a tearful farewell to his brother. Ramon stood by himself at the door of the church and waved back. Gradually the wagon disappeared into the distance. "*Vaya con Dios,*" he whispered. Go with God.

Ramon left Tío Pablo's squalid *casa* and moved into the church house with Padre Gutierrez, continuing his chores there but now also taking meals with the household and being given such clothing and personal items as he needed. He wrote letters to Luís every week, usually during math class when Don Armenta was not looking, and hoped someone was reading them to his brother.

He missed Luís very much. But as time passed, he gradually settled into his new life.

"THE bishop is coming! He's coming here to Meoqui!"

The news swept through the village. The bishop was traveling about the region and was to pass through Meoqui. An occasion such as this did not occur often, and was cause for great excitement. Some of the local folk who rarely left town, particularly the younger ones, had never even seen him before.

Ramon was kept quite busy as the church was made ready for the visit. Fresh beeswax was purchased and candles poured, linens and vestments were washed and starched, and flowers from Padre Gutierrez's own *patio* were brought into the church and carefully grouped into fragrant arrangements.

Ramon smiled fondly as he placed the roses and *yucca* flowers into vases and laid fresh palm fronds about the altar. This had been Mamá's task when she worked here, and Ramon could almost feel that she was still here with him. He sang and prayed as he worked, just as she had bid him to do.

He practiced poetry, too, for he was to recite *Ode to the Sacred Heart of Jesus* at the bishop's banquet the following night. He hoped he would not be too nervous to remember the words.

The next morning a *calesta* wagon, gaily decorated with ribbons and flowers, was dispatched to fetch the bishop, with several important townspeople arguing over who would have the honor of pulling it. The wagon returned later with their exalted guest. The church bell pealed out a joyous welcome as Ramon rang it with gusto, hurling his body weight down hard on the rope held tightly in his hands, and then being flung high into the air as the massive bell swung back.

The Mass was grand, as the villagers outdid themselves in showing their appreciation for the rare visit. A children's choir sang *Te Deum* and the bishop wore an embroidered stole made for him by the village women. Ramon served at the great banquet that followed the Mass, presenting platters of fruit and meat to His Grace and trying very hard not to spill wine as he poured it into fine goblets. He even rendered a flawless recitation of the *Ode*.

Mamá would be proud of me, he thought as he stood in a corner during a brief lull and ate a slice of pork. He licked the juice off his fingers and watched as a group of giggling children swung blindfolded at a bright *piñata*. One of them struck it and it burst, sending a shower of candies everywhere. With squeals of delight, the children fell to the floor and grabbed at the candy.

Ramon sighed. It was a grand *fiesta*, and Luís would have loved it. Ramon could only hope his little brother was enjoying his new life on the *hacienda*.

"Ramon! More wine here!" called Padre Gutierrez from the bishop's table, and, with a last look at the playing children, Ramon went to fetch the pitcher.

Next morning, amid a great ceremony, the bishop was sent on his way. The banquet was the talk of the town for days, with many of the poorer villagers having eaten better that night than they had in years.

One day many weeks later, Padre Gutierrez called Ramon into his office. He looked gravely at Ramon and began to speak.

"I am going away," he said, rising from his chair and going to the window. "It is one of the things the bishop and I discussed. He wishes to transfer me to another town."

What? Ramon could scarcely believe what he was hearing. Padre Gutierrez was going to be taken from him, too? Once again, Ramon felt the bitter injustice of his life. Although the *padre* was harsh in his occasional discipline, he had treated Ramon quite well, encouraging the boy in his studies and providing a stable home for him. And now Ramon found himself wondering yet again what his future was to be.

Leaving the window, with its view of his garden and beloved aviary, the *padre* went to his desk and withdrew a letter.

"I've written to your Tío Daniel, whose son is the foreman of El Gatiado *hacienda* where Luís is now living."

Ramon's heart leaped. Was he to be reunited with his brother?

The *padre's* next words confirmed Ramon's hope.

"Your *tío* does not wish for you to accompany me. He would prefer that you come and join your brother working for him on the *hacienda*."

So Ramon was to be reunited with Luís, but to do so he would have to say farewell to Padre Gutierrez. Although excited about seeing his brother again, it was with a heavy heart that Ramon climbed into the horse wagon that arrived later in the week for him. Life, he had learned, was full of goodbyes.

He'd hoped to see Luís right away upon reaching the *hacienda*, but was disappointed. The cart drove past the *casa's* grand entrance and around to the rear. The young girl who met him there told him that his brother was away washing the laundry. Slinging the satchel of his meager belongings over his shoulder, Ramon hopped down from the cart and followed the girl into the kitchen.

"I'm your cousin, Rosa," the girl said. She seemed to be slightly older than Ramon, and wore a simple cotton dress that had likely once been a gay blue but was now faded from much wear.

The kitchen was large, with a huge plank table. Rosa gestured for Ramon to sit at the table. It was nearly noon, and Ramon, hungry from the trip in the wagon, supposed he would be given a meal.

Instead, Rosa set a sack of mangoes before him and handed him a knife.

"Here," she said, reaching into a cupboard for a wooden bowl that she set on the table. "You can put the peels in there. When you're done peeling, cut the mangoes into small bits and mix them with this meat. Then call me."

Ramon must have looked dismayed, for Rosa, turning to him just as his stomach rumbled, said, "Oh, are you hungry? I suppose you can eat one of the mangoes, if you're quick about it."

Just then, two small children came clattering into the kitchen, yelling raucously as they charged through.

"Clara! Marco!" Rosa's voice was sharp as she disciplined the children. "No running inside!"

The rebuked children carried their noisy play into another room. Rosa shot Ramon a harried look and an apologetic smile.

"It's just that there's so much to do around here, and with my older sister married now there's no one left to mind the house and the children except me. But you'll be a big help, I know you will. *Ay*, Jorge!" Having tarried too long with Ramon, Rosa hastily snatched up two pails of scraps and went running to the door, pausing to shove it open with her hip before hurrying after a passing farm laborer.

Thus welcomed into the busy life of the *hacienda*, Ramon quickly slurped down a mango and bent to his task.

It was well into the afternoon before he saw Luís. The farm hands were returning from the fields in great carts, and the big kitchen began to fill up with husky men, sweaty and reeking from their day's labors and looking for food.

Under Rosa's guidance, Ramon had set two tables: the one there in the kitchen with a simple meal of beans and *tortillas* which the hungry men fell upon, and another, much grander table out on the shaded *patio*, set with linen napkins and silver cutlery, with candles and crystal goblets of wine, and savory roasts of pork and venison dripping juices onto their platters and basted with rich sauces. This was where the family would dine.

Rosa had changed into a finer dress and joined her family outside. Ramon could hear the sounds of clinking glass and conversation coming in through the window as he slid onto a bench beside the men at the kitchen table.

"Ramon! Ramon!" He heard a familiar voice and turned to see Luís running toward him. Leaping from the bench, Ramon met Luís halfway across the room and the two long-separated brothers threw their arms about each other.

"Oh, Ramon, it's so good to see you again!" Luís's voice was muffled against Ramon's shoulder. Pulling apart, the boys looked at each other with laughter and tears.

Seeing his little brother for the first time in over a year, Ramon was shocked at his appearance. In their time apart Luís had grown slightly taller, but was thinner than ever. And although his face had been tanned brown by the desert sun, there were dark circles under his eyes.

Trying not to let his dismay show, Ramon pummeled Luís spiritedly on the back, only to have the younger boy wince and pull away. Suddenly suspicious, Ramon flipped up the back of Luís's soiled white shirt and exposed his back, where the red weals of a recent whipping could be clearly seen.

As if to confirm his fears, Luís gently tugged Ramon away from the kitchen table, where the laborers were gobbling their food, and led him out into the blazing afternoon sun.

"Tío Daniel will be very angry if he catches you eating at the kitchen table," he explained. "Here." And Luís reached into a pocket and pulled out a piece of *tortilla* for Ramon to eat.

"I don't understand. Isn't that where the workers eat?" Ramon nodded toward the kitchen with its simple but filling fare of beans.

"It's where the *hired* workers eat," clarified Luís.

"But. . ." Ramon was puzzled. Had they not come here to work, too? "What does that make us?"

Luís's answer summed up their new life in one word.

"Orphans."

Chapter 13

THE *HACIENDA*

THE lowing of cattle in the corral outside the kitchen window awakened Ramon, with goats, horses, and roosters calling out in the background. In the chill darkness before dawn, he and Luís roused each other and yawned, stretching their sore muscles in anticipation of the day's labors. It was Ramon's second day at the hacienda.

They crept out from the warm fireplace ashes where they had slept and tiptoed around the farm workers slumbering on corn-husk mattresses scattered about the floor. Firewood was fetched, the hearth was kindled, and soon they were cooking breakfast.

Dawn had streaked the sky with pink and gold as Ramon, stirring beans in a large pot on the stove, was joined by Rosa, come to supervise the massive effort of feeding the hungry farmhands heading out to their labors. Later the family would come down to partake of their own leisurely repast. And then Ramon and Luís could begin their real chores.

Ramon supposed his life here was no worse than it had been with Tío Pablo. At least there was enough to eat, so long as Tío Daniel did not catch him pausing in his tasks to take the time to eat it.

Once the rowdy laborers had devoured their breakfast and departed, the smaller of the family's many children began to find their way into the kitchen, where they were constantly underfoot. At age fourteen, Rosa was the oldest, and had her hands full trying to keep her younger siblings out of mischief as she, Ramon, and Luís prepared the family's meal.

"He pulled my hair!"

"Well, she threw my toy gun out the window!"

"You were shooting me with it!"

"You're the outlaw Madero and I have to send you to jail."

"I'm going to tell Papá!"

"Vicente, don't pull your sister's hair. And you know better than to eavesdrop while Papá talks politics." Wearily passing a silver tray of sweet *pan de leche* bread to Ramon, Rosa went to fetch the play pistol while Ramon carried the tray outside to the dining table on the cool, shaded *patio*. In a corner of the kitchen, Luís stood churning butter while the youngest child, a boy of three, sat on the table, swinging his legs and flicking crumbs into Luís's face.

"I can't find my shirt!"

Returning from the *patio*, Ramon saw five-year-old Marco standing in the doorway, shirtless and wailing. Setting down the empty tray, Ramon went to the boy's room and found the shirt tossed behind a chair, only to return to the kitchen and discover that the boy was no longer there.

Soon Tío Daniel and his wife, the frail Tía Trinidad, had come downstairs and the family was gathered outside to dine in the cool morning air. Ramon breathed a sigh of relief, scraping bits of leftover egg and *chorizo* sausage onto *tortillas* for himself and Luís to eat. This they did quickly, while no one was watching, and then began to clean up the kitchen.

Scraps were tossed into the slop pail and the floor was carefully swept. Even here in the mountains, where it rained more frequently than in Meoqui, water was scarce, and dirty dishes were set aside to be taken later to a nearby lake where they would be scoured in sand and then rinsed.

Once breakfast was over and everything tidied up, he and Luís were assigned their chores for the day. Today they were to help Rosa with "women's work", and before long had been set to polishing the silver and the woodwork. They finished this in time to help their young cousin with the midday meal, after which they assisted her in various food-preparation tasks.

"Five groups of five equals twenty-five." Glancing about to make sure nobody had observed him, Ramon plucked up the twenty-five wheat kernels he'd placed in five neat piles on the floor beside him and dropped them into the *molcajeta* to be ground into flour.

"Pssst! What are you doing?" Luís hissed at him from the corner where he sat mixing sticky *tamale* dough in a large bowl. "You know if Tío Daniel catches you he'll clout you."

"I know." Ramon was unrepentant. He missed school terribly, even the math class he had so detested. But if he could just find opportunities to quiz himself, perhaps he would not forget his lessons. With determination, he constantly searched for chances such as this in which he could exercise his mind. Casting a furtive glance about to make sure there was still no one watching, he scooped out another handful of kernels.

"Nine groups of four make thirty-six."

"Besides, what difference does it make?" Luís paused to scrape sticky white dough from his fingers. "You'll never go to the university now."

"Six groups of—" Hearing his brother's words, Ramon faltered in the midst of counting out more kernels. There was truth to what Luís said, but the determined Ramon refused to listen. "Six groups. . . of. . . of eight. . ."

Hearing Rosa's footsteps approaching, he hastily swept up the kernels with his hand and dropped them into the stone *molcajeta*. Taking up the pestle, he ground energetically at them, crushing and grinding them into white flour.

"Have you finished yet?" the girl asked as she entered the kitchen. "Mamá wants to eat the *tamales* tonight, and we still have the laundry to do. We'll be heading up to the lake in about an hour, so be sure you're done mixing the dough by then. We'll have just enough time to steam them when we return." With that, their cousin dropped an armful of soiled aprons into the laundry basket and left them.

"Whew, that was close," said Luís.

"She wouldn't have done anything if she'd caught me. She's nice, even if she is bossy."

"Perhaps, but she might tell Tío Daniel or Don Alexandro."

Ramon had to agree with that. His cousin Alexandro was Tío Daniel's son, and the *hacienda's* harsh foreman. Ramon reluctantly ceased making piles of wheat on the floor. Then he had an idea.

"Here, Luís, let's try this. You make up a problem for me and I'll try to solve it."

Luís wrinkled his small brow. "I don't understand."

"You know, just make up a situation in which one would have to use math to solve it, like counting groups of cows or something."

"Oh, I see." Luís paused to add his dough to a larger bowl, and then looked about for more flour. "Have you finished grinding enough for me to make another batch?"

Tipping over the heavy stone *molcajeta*, Ramon dumped the flour into Luís's mixing bowl as Luís carefully measured out more lard. They worked in silence for a few minutes, and then Luís spoke.

"OK, I have one. Fifteen people will be eating supper and they will each have three *tamales*. How many *tamales* do we need to prepare?"

Ramon chuckled. Fifteen people *would* be eating supper later that evening, and would likely have three *tamales* each. Was Luís giving him a subtle hint that they needed to work faster? Ramon had never suspected his little brother of having a sense of humor!

"That's easy. We need to make forty-five *tamales*, and yes it's a lot. But don't worry, we'll finish in time. Now give me another problem."

They continued making dough and doing arithmetic for the next hour until Rosa came to fetch them. After cleaning up and setting the dough where it would remain cool, they each took up baskets of laundry and dirty dishes and proceeded to the lake.

Even Tío Daniel was not rich enough to spend money on soap for the washing of clothes; the only soap in the house was perfumed and meant for the washing of ladies' faces. Instead, *lechugilla*, the roots of palm trees, were dug up and boiled in a metal tub along with the laundry. Both the *lechugilla* and the tub were stored in a shed by the lake, along with some wood for the fire.

Within minutes, Rosa had kindled a blaze beside the lake, and the tub was filled with water and the clothes set to boiling. She stayed to mind the clothes, while Ramon rolled up the ends of his pants and washed dishes along the water's edge. Meanwhile, Luís went off to collect more of the scrubby mesquite and creosote bushes to be cut for firewood, as the supply in the shed was running low.

The afternoon sun blazed down, but the lake's water cooled Ramon off and he began to enjoy his task. Letting his mind wander, he thought back to his school days.

" *'Double, double, toil and trouble.'* " The boiling laundry put him in mind of Shakespeare's three sinister witches. " *'Fire burn and cauldron bubble.'* "

"What's that?" Hot from her labor at the fire, Rosa had come to join Ramon for a quick break at the cool water.

"Oh, it's nothing," Ramon hastened to assure her, concerned lest she feel he was slacking in his work. "Just some poetry I learned in school."

His cousin did not seem inclined to censure him, and even looked up in mild interest.

"Uh, it's by an English man called Shakespeare." Encouraged, Ramon continued: " *'Eye of newt and toe of frog, wool of bat and tongue of dog.'* "

Rosa smiled. "That's nice, I like it. You're lucky you were able to continue your schooling. I only got to learn reading and writing."

"I hope to go to the university when I'm older."

His cousin smiled at this and gently shook her head.

"You can't go to the university. My *papá* won't let you. I hear how he talks about you, and see how he treats you. You're an orphan. You're nobody, worth less than the ignorant *campesino* field hands he hires. You receive no pay. How will you be accepted into the university with no money, hmm?"

She spoke without spite, merely informing Ramon of the dreary facts of his life. But her words angered him.

"I will go!" he retorted hotly. "I will receive an education and earn good wages and then come back for Luís so we can go live in America!"

"America? My *papá* talks often of America. He has a cousin living there who sends us money and gifts."

Ramon knew this, for he was often present when the deliveries arrived. The books, paintings and other fine items arriving at the *hacienda* from the United States merely strengthened his determination to someday begin a life of his own in that wondrous country.

But Rosa was right. He had no way to pay for the education he'd need to obtain a good job. And so how would he possibly support himself and Luís in a new country?

Discouraged, he trudged with the others back to the big *casa* to prepare forty-five *tamales* for the family's supper. Then, after sharing a hasty meal of leftover meat scraps with Luís, he set about his evening chores and later crawled wearily into the sooty hearth with his brother. Tomorrow was going to be an exhausting day, for he was to accompany the men out into the fields. Yawning mightily, he was soon fast asleep.

Chapter 14

"WE MUST LEAVE"

CRASH! The whip came slashing down on Ramon's back, ripping into his already ragged shirt and sending fiery pain through the bleeding skin. Ramon bit his lip and tried not to cry out.

"You're not keeping up with the others!" The whip slashed down again as Don Alexandro struck at him from where he sat astride his horse Diablo.

Ramon cowered, scowling bitterly, not daring to stand up until the horse's whinnies grew fainter and he knew the man had moved on.

It wasn't that Ramon was not working hard. But the field hands were grown men who could easily heft the large sacks and carry them to the wagon, while Ramon had to drag his across the field. Often the delicate vegetable plants were crushed along the way as he did so, which merited another whipping.

The hot sun beat down, and while the men were permitted a drink break, Ramon was kept toiling. From the slight shade of the *sombrero* on his head, he enviously watched the men as they laughed and splashed.

The vast crop fields of El Gatiado were kept well-watered thanks to The Tank, an immense cistern at the base of the mountain where water, flowing down from the rugged *sierra*, was collected for irrigation. A shout from Don Alexandro riding past on Diablo signaled a halt to the laborers' break. The men began to fill pails with water amid much laughter and playful roughhousing as they set the pails onto a cart for distribution among the parched crops.

He never whips the hired campesinos, Ramon noted bitterly. The man was quick to use the whip to lash Ramon or Luís, yet he used the instrument merely to punctuate his commands to the others, cracking it harmlessly in the air. He even tolerated the men's horseplay, provided they got their work done. But if he caught the two boys so much as sharing a joke, down came the whip on their backs.

With a feeling of relief, Ramon muscled his last sack of beets into the cart and went to go join his brother. In the patchy shade of a grape arbor, Luís was doggedly butchering the carcass of a large deer, carefully covering the cuts of meat with damp palm fronds to keep them from drying out. Taking up a knife, Ramon bent to assist him.

"Two steaks divided among eight people." Luís greeted him with whispered words and a quiet smile, after first glancing hastily about to make sure Don Alexandro was nowhere nearby.

Ramon smiled at the diversion. School might be a lost dream, but he was still eager to seize any opportunity to exercise his mind.

"That's easy. A quarter steak per person." Not that the family would tolerate such a scanty portion! Better to grind the meat for *tacos*; it would go a lot farther. Sighing wistfully, for a quarter steak would be a feast for him, he helped his brother slice up the remainder of the meat.

It was cold that night, for even in the desert the autumn temperature could drop to freezing, especially in the mountains. Ramon woke around midnight, shivering, with Luís sleeping fitfully beside him. The coals in the hearth had died out.

Tío Daniel and his family were all asleep in their bedrooms upstairs, and judging from the snores, the field hands here in the kitchen slept soundly on their corn husk pallets. Crossing his fingers that he would not be caught, Ramon quietly slipped out the kitchen door to the woodshed and gathered up a small armload of mesquite kindling.

Hastening back inside, he coaxed Luís out of the hearth and stirred up the fire. The hearth warmed rapidly, and the two boys curled up on the hard floor before it and were soon fast asleep.

But the price of their night's sleep was a sound lashing the following morning.

"There's firewood missing from the kitchen shed! Did you take it?" Don Alexandro had followed Ramon and Luís out to the lake where he proceeded to mete out his harsh discipline, savagely whipping them both until Luís collapsed sobbing onto the ground. "You will cut wood and stock the shed until it won't hold one more stick! *After* you finish your day's chores!" With that, he spurred his horse and rode away, leaving Ramon to comfort his little brother.

"Why is he so mean to us?" sniffled Luís. "What's wrong with being orphans? It's not our fault Mamá and Papá are gone."

Ramon had no answer for that, but one thought was suddenly clear in his mind: He and his brother could no longer stay there.

"We must leave this place," he said.

"Where would we go?" The novelty of this idea chased away the last of Luís's tears and he looked up at Ramon with wide eyes.

"I don't know." Ramon thought hard. Padre Gutierrez was gone from Meoqui, leaving only Tío Pablo, who would treat them just as poorly as Don Alexandro did. There was Tía Lola in the city, and also Tía Lupe, but their husbands would not permit them to take the boys in. He and his brother really were all alone.

Two nights later, Tío Daniel and Tía Trinidad were invited to dine at a neighboring *hacienda* and took Rosa with them, instructing Ramon to stay and care for the children.

"Tonight's our chance!" he said to Luís. Together they prepared the usual bean supper for the *campesinos* and fed the children *enchiladas* with *mole poblano*. Then later, once they had taken the children upstairs to their beds and tucked them in, they waited for the *campesinos* to flop onto their corn husk pallets and go to sleep.

Stuffing a satchel with fruit and meat, Ramon quietly gestured for Luís to follow him, and the two tiptoed through the kitchen door and out into the night. Unsure where to go, with just the moon and stars to guide them, they could only hope that they would find themselves someplace kinder than the home they were leaving.

They headed out toward the lake, then past The Tank and up the mountain. Within an hour, they were well into the great desert wilderness of the Sierra Madre, journeying past short barrel cactuses, and tall, thorny acacia trees. These and other things cast eerie leaping shadows at them in the moonlight.

"What was that?" cried Luís in alarm at a piercing sound issuing from the darkness.

"It's only an owl," Ramon assured him, clutching more tightly at his brother's small hand and hoping it *was* just an owl. The desert at night was not a friendly place. "Here, let's stop for a moment and have something to eat."

Nervously, not daring to sit down, the boys chewed meat with mouths too dry to properly enjoy it. They carelessly tossed the bones into the darkness, then froze as something unseen was heard nearby.

"Let's get out of here!"

Cramming the rest of the meat back into the satchel, they hurried away as fast as the darkness permitted.

Before long, Luís began to get cold. Pulling Luís closed to himself, Ramon slowed his step to match the younger boy's, and together they continued to trudge through the night.

"Look!" said Luís sometime later. "Let's stop there for the night." He was pointing to a craggy knob of sandstone that poked up out of the ground. "We could light a fire."

Ramon eyed the rocks dubiously, thinking of all manner of creatures that might inhabit such a place. But Luís was shivering, and Ramon knew he had to protect his brother from the cold.

He gathered up what few sticks and twigs he could find, but try as he might he could not get a fire started.

"We have no tinder," he muttered to himself, wishing there were *piñon* trees nearby with their sticky, resinous pine cones that easily caught sparks. But at least Luís had stopped shivering and was even beginning to doze off, huddled against the rocks that reflected back some of their body heat.

Ramon, also very sleepy, kicked aside his failed attempt at a fire and curled up beside Luís, pressing his cheek against the sandstone that still retained some of the day's warmth. He had almost drifted off to sleep when a stab of alarm bolted through him. Something had crawled over his arm!

Ugh! He sat straight up and brushed wildly at his arm, making sure whatever it was had not crept down his shirt.

"Luís! Wake up!"

"Mmm? Wha. . . what is it?" Luís muzzily blinked his eyes and rolled over.

"I think there might be a snake!" Ramon pulled away from the knob's stony crevices, straining to hear the telltale rustlings of any small creature, or worse, the rattle of an angry snake. "Be, very still!"

The moon was high in the night sky, and the desert, having slumbered through the sizzling heat of day, was now filled with the sounds of activity. Ramon knew that many kinds of animals lived in these mountains, including jackrabbits, lizards, bats, deer, sheep, and even wolves and mountain lions. And woven through the chill darkness was the ever-present musical calling of distant coyotes.

The night sounds were pleasant in their own way. Having reassured himself that no rattlers were nearby, Ramon found himself again nodding off.

Then the peaceful night was split by a scream that turned Ramon's blood to ice. *Mountain lion!*

Beside him, Luís gasped and jerked awake.

"Ramon! Ramon! Was that a—?"

Horrified, Ramon's mind raced. "The meat! It must smell the meat!" Snatching up the satchel of food, he flung it as far into the darkness as he could, then grabbed Luís's hand and yanked the small boy to his feet.

"Come on! Run!"

"Where?" Luís stumbled clumsily as he was pulled along.

"Away from here!" The last thing Ramon wished was to be anywhere near a feeding mountain lion.

In their terror, the two boys pelted through the moonlit desert, kicking up sand and scratching their ankles in the cactuses and scrubby brush until, too exhausted to run any more, they collapsed in a weary heap beneath the starry sky.

That is where Don Alexandro found them the next morning.

Chapter 15

KIND SEÑOR OAXACA

RAMON jerked awake. So many things were happening at once that his mind reeled. He heard the familiar, dreaded crack of Don Alexandro's whip, the anguished wail of his little brother, and the scream of defiance from an enraged horse.

Blinking in confusion as he struggled to rouse, Ramon saw Luís bolting across the desert toward the sunrise, with Tío Daniel galloping after him and Don Alexandro astride a wildly rearing Diablo, struggling to remain seated. A scrawny *burro* stood hunched off to one side.

"*Ay*, you'd better run!" Viciously stabbing his spurs into the flanks of the stallion as he tried to regain control, Don Alexandro yelled furiously after Luís. "You'd better run, because when I get my hands on you. . ."

With savage force, Don Alexandro muscled Diablo to a standstill. Then, angered that his inability to control the beast had been witnessed by Ramon, he leaped from the horse's back and lashed with his whip at the cowering boy.

"How dare you run away, you orphan *mocoso!* We've been looking for you two all night."

Through the numbing pain of the whip, Ramon's mind churned. How had the family learned of their disappearance? He supposed they must have returned from their visit and wished to awaken the boys to perform some late-night task, only to discover that they were not asleep in their customary spot. More puzzling: how had they located the runaways?

As if reading Ramon's thoughts, Don Alexandro flung something at him which landed on the ground with a heavy thud. From it came the buzz of flies and the stench of spoiled meat.

"We found this not far from here, and knew you were nearby. So now you've stolen from us, eh?"

Ramon just had time to see the familiar satchel, now bloodied and ripped from its night among the animals, before being yanked to his feet. "Found a mountain lion, I see. Well, I'd as soon leave you here for him to eat if I didn't need you so badly to work in my fields."

With that, the man snatched up a coil of rope hung from Diablo's saddle, and before Ramon knew what was happening he found himself tied firmly hand and foot. His struggles were useless as he was tossed over the *burro's* back like a sack of corn.

Not satisfied that Ramon was securely bound, the big man then hefted his whip and lashed it mercilessly at Ramon as he lay helpless over the *burro,* until both boy and animal cried out in pain. Then, without another word, Don Alexandro remounted and wheeled Diablo about, heading back to El Gatiado with his captive.

Utterly dejected, Ramon bounced head down over the *burro's* back all the way to the *hacienda.* Exhausted from the cold night on the mountain, and shaken by his violent recapture this morning, his weary brain could formulate no plan of action. So when Don Alexandro reined to a halt beside the lake and cut Ramon's bonds, what happened next came as much as a surprise to himself as to anyone else. He leaped to his feet and went running into the lake.

"*Ay, caramba!* You get back here!" Fuming at this unexpected turn of events, the man stood helplessly at the water's edge and shook his fist in the air. "I'll make you wish you'd never been born!" Taking a few hesitant steps into the water, he seemed about to swim after Ramon, but evidently decided it was not worth the effort.

Turning around, he trudged back out of the lake and poured water from his boots, then strode angrily in the direction of the *casa*.

Ramon, meanwhile, was suddenly remembering why he had never ventured out into the lake before now: he could not swim. His initial frenzy had waned, leaving him thrashing about in water over his head and becoming weaker by the minute. He knew he could not remain there much longer. Yet to return to the *hacienda* would be to meekly accept Don Alexandro's abuse. And for how long? Would he and Luís have to spend the rest of their lives lashed to bloody bits? Ramon's mind quailed at the notion.

He sank below the water, then summoned the strength to fight his way to the surface again, where he gasped mightily for air. His arms burned from the effort of his flailing. Maybe it would be better to just sink into the water and stay there, to end the misery of his life.

No! Even as he sank again below the surface, his fierce determination asserted itself. Jesus would not wish him to simply give up, and neither would Mamá. He had dreams, hopes that were worth fighting for. Going to school, living in America. Besides, someone must look after Luís.

It was this last thought that galvanized him. He could not, *would* not, abandon his little brother. Spurred to one final desperate effort, he grappled his way from the depths and gulped at the life-giving air.

Please, Jesus, the despairing boy prayed as he floundered his way out of the lake to collapse dripping on the muddy shore, *send me an angel, for I am all alone and don't know what to do.*

The hot desert sun warmed his torn skin as he lay there. He could smell the scent of mesquite smoke on the breeze, and in the distance he could hear the lowing of cattle, and. . . something else, too: clip-clopping hoofbeats. Scarcely daring to hope, Ramon looked up and saw that an angel had indeed come.

"Señor Oaxaca!" Staggering to his feet, Ramon lurched away from the lake's edge. Relief gave strength to his wobbly legs until he was racing over the ground, past grazing goats and out to the main road where the gentleman was passing by in his fine horse carriage, driving to El Gatiado on one of his periodic visits to inspect the *hacienda* he owned.

Without stopping to think that he was dripping wet and smeared with mud, with his skin slashed and bleeding from the morning's whipping, Ramon ran with waving arms out into the road.

Halting the horses, Señor Oaxaca stepped down from the carriage to see what was amiss. Ramon, a grown boy pushed beyond the brink of human endurance, flung his arms around the astonished man and burst into tears.

"REALLY, Daniel, this simply won't do." Señor Oaxaca took a puff on his cigar before continuing. "That boy is bright. I remember him from the school in Meoqui. Read a poem for the bishop, he did." Señor Oaxaca chuckled and raised the cigar to his lips for another fragrant puff. "He shouldn't be in the fields at all, and he certainly shouldn't be lashed to within an inch of his life."

"He ran away!" Tío Daniel felt compelled to defend his son Alexandro's actions.

"Why? Has he cause to be unhappy here?" Señor Oaxaca gave Tío Daniel a hard look. Tío Daniel said nothing.

Señor Oaxaca stubbed out his cigar and sighed. "I knew your field hands were worked hard and paid little, but since they seemed satisfied I was willing to overlook it. This beating of the orphans, however, will not be tolerated." He grew silent for a bit, pondering the situation, then spoke again.

"This is what I am going to do. Ramon will come with me. He needs a doctor. Those slashes are deep and need disinfectant and stitches." The gentleman scowled as he recalled gently pulling back Ramon's tattered shirt and finding the fresh wounds as well as the poorly healed scars from past beatings. "He will remain with me. I shall be staying at my villa in the city for several months, and will see that he attends the school there and finds employment in his free time.

"You, Daniel, will have someone tend to the boy Luís. Give him rest and good food until his own wounds heal, and then see that he works only in the kitchen, under the supervision of your daughter Rosa. He is never again to be beaten, do I make myself clear?"

Cowed, Tío Daniel merely nodded, while Señor Oaxaca rose from his comfortable chair and went to the upstairs bedroom where Ramon lay shivering on soft cotton sheets.

Ramon's wet, torn clothing had been removed and warm pads applied to his back. He lay on his stomach, with an anxious Luís by his side, while

Señor Oaxaca spoke gently to him of the new arrangement.

"We will not be living very far from here," he explained. "I will instruct your *tío* to permit Luís some free time from his chores to come and visit you." This brought a smile to Ramon's face, and Luís positively beamed at the thought of spending time away from the *hacienda*. And when Señor Oaxaca told Ramon that he was to return to school, Ramon was so overcome with joy that he nearly cried again.

Later that week, he sat beside Señor Oaxaca in the horse carriage as it rolled away from El Gatiado. Luís waved, a forlorn figure standing there alone, and Ramon took comfort from knowing his brother would be well-treated now. Things were again changing, this time, he hoped, for the better.

Señor Oaxaca's villa was located in the heart of Chihuahua, not far from the great cathedral where Ramon had made his First Holy Communion. And there was the Alameda, where he and Josefita had sold candy on Sunday afternoons. He wondered if she still did so, and whether he would see her again.

By the end of the week Ramon's back was healed, and Señor Oaxaca had spoken to his old teacher Don Armenta about the boy's return to school. Ramon was given his very own room at Señor Oaxaca's villa, with a real bed and fresh cotton sheets, and a shelf of books, and even a little desk where he could sit and study.

Although he did not dine with the *señor*, there was always plenty to eat, with carts of fruit, cheeses, and meats arriving weekly from El Gatiado. Sometimes Luís accompanied the carts, and the two boys would spend precious time together.

But other times it would be Tío Daniel who came with the cart, and Ramon had learned that on those days it was best to stay away.

The first time Tío Daniel had come to the villa, Ramon had been out on the *patio* doing his homework. A shadow fell over him and he looked up to see his *tío* standing there.

"Studying hard, I see."

A slight wariness crept over Ramon. "*Sí, señor*," he replied, wondering why his *tío* was addressing him.

"You go to school every day?"

"*Sí, señor*. Except for Saturday and Sunday."

"Do you have a job?"

Ramon began to see where this conversation was heading, and wished Señor Oaxaca were home.

"I milk cows, *señor*. For one of Señor Oaxaca's friends. Every morning and afternoon."

"And you are paid for this?"

Ramon did not want to answer, but neither did he want to anger his *tío*. "*Sí*," he was finally forced to admit.

Reaching suddenly forward, Tío Daniel grabbed Ramon by the arm so hard that the startled boy dropped his book.

"Give me the money. You owe it to me, for I am family."

Ramon grew alarmed. Surely Tío Daniel was not about to strike him? Here, in Señor Oaxaca's own *home?*

Just then Señor Oaxaca's dog, a great St. Bernard named Caesar, came loping out of the villa onto the *patio* and halted before Tío Daniel, baring his teeth in a warning growl. Releasing Ramon's arm, Tío Daniel began stepping slowly back. When he reached the brick path that led from the *patio* through an arch and out to the street, he turned with one last glower at Ramon and strode away.

Later that evening when Señor Oaxaca had returned, Ramon related the incident to him. The gentleman lit a cigar and sat back to give the matter some thought, then spoke.

"He is right, you know. No!" he added hastily, seeing Ramon's sudden fear. "Not to take your money by force. But," and he puffed on the cigar, "he is your *tío*. Your mother's brother, *sí?* Well, point is, he's family, and he is providing a home for Luís. Since you're earning wages now, you really should contribute on your brother's behalf."

Grudgingly, Ramon supposed this was fair. "Contribute how much?"

Señor Oaxaca shrugged. "One *centavo?* I can instruct your employer to withhold it from your wages in an account that will be paid directly to Daniel. This way he will have no reason to attempt extorting it from you."

Ramon agreed, trusting Señor Oaxaca to make the arrangements. He knew the man was honest. Ramon had even, upon first coming to live with him, shown him the small pouch of coins he'd retrieved from under the cactus at Tío Pablo's. Señor Oaxaca had smiled and told Ramon to keep the pouch in his room, which the boy did, adding to it every week as he was paid.

The pouch continued to grow fatter as the weeks went by. Luís, on his occasional visits, assured his brother that the whippings had stopped and that he was allowed to eat his fill at the kitchen table with the other workers. He worked hard for Rosa, and she was kind to him.

And Ramon continued to do well in school, excelling even in the math he had once so hated. He had to smile whenever he recalled having multiplied *tamales* and divided steaks in his head so he would not forget how.

Tío Daniel came often to speak to Señor Oaxaca concerning business affairs at El Gatiado. Ramon would usually retreat to his room to study on these occasions, but one day while in the kitchen he happened to overhear part of a conversation which stopped him in his tracks. Intrigued, he boldly crept toward a window overlooking the *patio* where the two men sat, so that he could hear more clearly.

"You'll be sorely missed, Daniel," he heard Señor Oaxaca say. "El Gatiado has prospered under your management. I assume you'll be promoting your son to overseer in your place?"

"*Sí, señor*. Alexandro will run the *hacienda* well. He has been training one of his men to take over as field foreman."

Ramon, crouching beside the window, gasped in surprise. Tío Daniel was leaving El Gatiado? Why? And where was he going?

Hoping no one had heard him, he edged closer to the window, eager to learn more.

"I'd like to take the orphan with me," continued Tío Daniel.

"Which orphan? You mean Luís?"

"Well, yes, certainly him. He's small, but there will be much work to do and I'll need anybody I can get. But I meant the other one, Ramon."

Oh no! Ramon couldn't believe what he was hearing. Tío Daniel was planning to take him and Luís somewhere? Someplace where there would be 'much work to do'? No! Ramon wouldn't go. He'd run away again, take Luís with him and run someplace far away where Tío Daniel could never find them.

Stunned by what he had heard, and trying fiercely to plan what to do next, Ramon sank into a chair at the kitchen table and stared blankly into the air, one thought after another spinning through his mind.

"There you are." Ramon, lost in his thoughts, had not heard Tío Daniel enter the kitchen. Now the man stood beside the table, looming over

Ramon as he spoke. "I knew you were around somewhere. You're to come with me, not today, but in a week or so. I'll be back to fetch you."

Tío Daniel looked down at Ramon, sitting there in a chair in the comfortable sunny kitchen, and sneered. "You think you're so smart, don't you, with your schooling and your books. Well, there will be none of that where we're going. It's back to the field with you. Looks like you might come in handy after all, you and your brother both.

"My cousin's *hacienda* is not doing well. He needs someone to oversee the management, and he needs more laborers. I'm to be the overseer, and I'll be bringing some of my men to work the fields. And you, of course, because you can work for free." He laughed, a cruel sound, and Ramon, cringing at the thought of again toiling under a harsh whip, almost missed his next words.

"The *hacienda* is called Bella Vista. It is in America."

Chapter 16

THE JOURNEY BEGINS

RAMON'S jaw fell open and he sat speechless. America! He could not believe what he had just heard. He was going to America! He sat, staring dumbfounded at his *tío*, while a hundred thoughts whirled around in his brain.

He was going to America. His mind boggled at this. No more plotting and scheming! No more saving his *pesos* to try and get into the university! He needn't spend years educating himself in order to get a fine job to earn the money necessary to finance a life across the border, because Tío Daniel was simply *taking* him there. To America. As simple as that. His heart's dream of a life in America was going to come true, right now.

"Señor Oaxaca!" Leaping to his feet, Ramon went running out onto the *patio*, barely able to contain his joy. "*Señor*, I'm going to America!"

Furious at the boy's insolence, Tío Daniel came storming out the door after him. The great St. Bernard dog, Caesar, resting at his master's feet, raised his alert head at the commotion and gave a slight growl. Startled, Tío Daniel kicked belligerently at the dog.

This was a mistake. Caesar instantly leaped to his feet, and before Señor Oaxaca could call the dog off, it had lunged directly at Tío Daniel. Without thinking, Ramon flung out his arms to shield his *tío* from the attack.

Piercing pain clamped down on the boy's arm and he was knocked spinning to the *patio*. Cool tile pressed against his cheek as above him he heard roars of confusion, from Señor Oaxaca, from Tío Daniel, and even from poor, bewildered Caesar. Shoving hard at the furry mass holding him down, Ramon clambered to his feet in time to see his disgusted Tío Daniel spluttering away while Señor Oaxaca, risen now from his comfortable leather chair, laid a firm hand on the dog's head.

Turning his attention to the dazed boy, the kind *señor* gently took Ramon's hand and bent to examine his wounded arm.

"He's a hard one, your *tío* is," he said as he led Ramon into the *casa*. Taking down some iodine, he ministered the arm as he continued. "He's told you what he plans?"

"*Sí, señor*. This is what I was coming to tell you." But the shock of the sudden attack had knocked the excitement out of Ramon, and it was slowly being replaced by a vague sense of unease.

As if reading the boy's thoughts, Señor Oaxaca said, "Do you understand what it will mean?"

The reality of the situation became clear to Ramon. He was to go live in America, but he would pay a heavy price, indeed, for this opportunity: not in *pesos* but in human suffering. *Much work to do*, his *tío* had said, and already Ramon could anticipate the lashings, the long hours he would be expected to toil in the hot sun on meager rations, the general abuse he would receive.

"Daniel will be leaving my employ, and so I will no longer be able to govern his custody of you and your brother. I know nothing of his cousin, and it may be that this man will treat you boys fairly, but you must accept that, for the time being at least, it may fall to you to endure whatever will come.

"And yet," the man continued, lighting a cigar and leading the bandaged Ramon back out onto the *patio*, "I suspect that a bright boy like you can turn an opportunity such as this to your advantage." Sinking into his great leather chair and pouring two glasses of cold wine, he offered one to Ramon and gestured for the boy to sit as well. "You remind me a great deal of myself at your age, you know. I'd hoped to provide you with the chance to better yourself through education, as I did, but it seems this is not to be.

"However, all may not be lost. Growing up in America, there will doubtless be various other avenues open to you. Work hard for your *tío*, remember always the suffering of Jesus, and I have every confidence that one day you will achieve success."

Ramon appreciated this candid advice. He knew he would greatly miss Señor Oaxaca, a true gentleman who was not too grand to sit with an orphan boy, a boy who showed promise of becoming a man such as himself. Ramon was reminded of Padre Gutierrez in Meoqui, one who had likewise believed in him and offered a chance for him to fulfill his potential.

I won't let them down, he vowed silently. In America anything was possible, even happiness for a pair of lonely orphan boys.

The next days were a blur for Ramon. Before returning to El Gatiado to help with preparations, he said goodbye to his friends in the school and to Don Armenta, knowing that this time it was for good. He even went to visit Tía Lupe and his cousin Josefita, who at age fourteen was becoming a lovely young *señorita*.

"Remember the afternoons we spent here selling candy and watching the bicycles?" she asked as they walked through the Alameda.

Ramon smiled at the pleasant memory. "Do you still?" he wondered.

"Oh, no." Josefita shook her head, sending ripples down her long dark hair. "I mostly come here now with Hector. My friend Elena accompanies us as my *dueña*," she continued, using the word for a lady who watches over a courting couple. "She says Hector will soon be asking to marry me, but *I* say he must wait until I'm fifteen."

Josefita was growing up. Ramon supposed he was, too. He hoped it wouldn't take too long.

"It's a shame I won't be able to complete my schooling," he said. "What sort of jobs do you think America will have for people like me?" Since he could read and write, perhaps he could find work someday at a newspaper.

Just then a man on horseback came riding through the tranquil Alameda, pausing only to nail a broadsheet to a cottonwood tree.

"*Viva* Madero!" he cried, making the horse rear onto its hind legs. "*Viva* Mexico!"

A crowd quickly gathered to read the broadsheet as the man rode away, and Ramon and Josefita joined them.

"I think it is well that you are leaving now," said Josefita, shivering slightly. "Ever since President Díaz rigged the election and arrested Madero, there's been nothing but trouble."

Ramon nodded, still staring at the photo of the outlaw on the broadsheet. "We learned in school that it was President Díaz who brought the railway to Mexico, and the telegraph, as well as oil and electricity. But none of those things help anybody but the rich. The food shipped out on those trains is picked by poor people, and they're paid almost nothing. Their homes have no electricity."

Josefita agreed. "Madero could have helped us. He believed power should not stay in the hands of Díaz's rich friends, but belongs to the people. If he ever comes back from exile, there may be fighting."

Fighting. Yes, Ramon could believe this. Even in tiny Meoqui, and later at El Gatiado, he had heard how the country folk of Mexico were rallying to the cause of their champion Francisco Madero. Imprisoned by the angry president, he had recently escaped and was calling for the people to rise in revolution and overthrow Díaz.

Tension ran high at El Gatiado, as well, as the family prepared to leave.

"You must be vigilant in the days to come," Tío Daniel counseled Don Alexandro. "If that idiot Madero succeeds in his bid for power, he may well attempt to 'liberate' this *hacienda*." He spat in disgust. "You'll have your hands full trying to keep the workers from deserting to go join him. And if it looks like there will be fighting. . . well, just leave and come to us at Bella Vista."

Wasn't that *deserting?* Ramon wondered with a snort as he filled a trunk with Rosa's cookware. The hypocrisy implied by Tío Daniel's suggestion that Don Alexandro abandon Señor Oaxaca's *hacienda* in its hour of need filled him with scorn.

The trunk, along with many others, was loaded into a wagon, and when the big day finally arrived, Ramon clambered aboard with Luís, Rosa, the children, and three *campesino* field hands who would be coming with them to work at Bella Vista.

"It's in a part of America called New Mexico," Ramon explained to Luís.

"Will we be there soon?"

"I don't think so. I heard Tío Daniel say we'll go first to the city of Juarez, along the border, to stay with a friend of his. We may be there for a while."

"Why?"

Ramon glanced over at Rosa, who shrugged.

"I don't know. Maybe it's not safe for us to cross the border just now."

He could hear Tía Trinidad's frail voice as Tío Daniel helped her into the front seat of the wagon. Moments later, Tío Daniel was aboard, too. With a crack of the whip and a creaking lurch, the wagon rolled forward. Ramon could scarcely contain his excitement. The first step had been taken in their journey to America!

Several uneventful days passed on the hot, dusty road to Juarez, until finally they were passing through the outskirts of the great sprawling city. It was *big*, much bigger than Chihuahua. There were *cantinas* on every street, and soldiers, too, big, rough-looking men with guns. The narrow lanes were so choked with people and *burro*-carts that Tío Daniel had to halt the wagon several times to let them pass.

A gasp from Luís caught Ramon's attention.

"Look!" Luís was pointing down the street. Ramon, Rosa, the children, and the *campesinos* all turned where they sat in the wagon bed to look where Luís was pointing, and their eyes grew big.

Chapter 17

AMERICA AT LAST

"IT'S an automobile!" cried one of the children.

"It must belong to somebody rich!" said another, as the sleek black motor car bounced past on the rutted street. The driver, seated in the low, open cockpit, was cursing and squeezing impatiently on a horn as he passed. People in the crowd darted this way and that to get out of his way, and slowly the automobile lumbered off down the street.

It was growing late when Tío Daniel at last pulled up to the home where they would be staying. Ramon and Luís helped the fieldhands unload the wagon while the family went inside to be introduced to their host. Then the boys went to join Rosa in the kitchen.

The *casa*, one of several in a prosperous neighborhood of the city, was small, and it was obvious that while Tío Daniel's friend was most generous to have offered them hospitality as they awaited entry into the United States, his resources would be stretched a bit thin.

To help with this, Ramon and Luís, and Rosa, too, would be assisting the cook. After the first few awkward days, they became accustomed to their new roles, with Rosa helping to do the food preparation, Luís doing scullery chores, and Ramon acting primarily as errand boy. Unlike the *hacienda* El Gatiado, this *casa* in the city produced no crops, and so food and supplies needed to be purchased daily.

This arrangement was quite agreeable to Ramon. Frustrated at being just across the border from America yet waiting to enter, he at least found satisfaction in his freedom to roam about the vast, exciting city. Every morning, list in hand and basket over his arm, he would set out in search of the necessary merchants, vendors, and shopkeepers, until before long it had become familiar routine.

Milk and eggs. Today was Monday, a lovely October morning, and his first stop would be at Señor Fuentes's stall to buy the week's dairy items. Then lard from the butcher, flour and beans from the dry goods shop, and fresh fruit on the way home.

"*Hola*, Ramon!"

"*Hola*, Carlos!" Ramon, trotting down the dirt street, waved to the little neighbor boy playing in the dust. Further down the street Señora Eugenia was sprinkling water over the roses she coaxed to grow in the baked soil.

"*Hola*, Ramon! What a beautiful morning, *sí?*" she called as he sailed past her low *adobe* wall.

"*Sí, señora!*" he answered gaily, reaching out without breaking his stride to catch the rose she tossed to him.

Rounding the corner, he darted into an alleyway to avoid the *casa* of Señor Baca, who would fire a gun at anyone disturbing his prize roosters. Then back out into the sunlight and past a garbage heap on the side of the road. Flies buzzed around it, and Ramon held his rose under his nose to block out the stench.

The *adobe* homes about him crowded closer together now, and harsh city noises grew louder and more immediate as they echoed from the walls along the narrow road. Dogs prowled the streets and alleyways, scrawny, starving things with no owners.

His reflexes attuned by now to the energetic bustle of the city, Ramon felt vibrations through the thin leather soles of his *huaraches* even before he heard a wagon come bounding along. He leaped nimbly aside to let it race past, one of dozens clattering about the marketplace ahead.

Bells in the nearby cathedral were just beginning to ring as Ramon arrived at the main avenue, which was filled now with people going to and from the market. He paused a moment to scan the crowd, then smiled and hastened forward as he spotted a familiar pair seated on a bench.

"You're running late today, Ramon," the lady greeted him. "Chico and I were wondering if we'd missed you."

"Why, Señora Perez, you know you are the sunshine of my day. And Chico, too!" He bent to lift the tiny dog from its basket and held him close to receive an enthusiastic face-licking. Then Ramon held out his rose with a flourish. "For you, lovely *señora*."

"*Muchas gracias*." Tucking the rose into her

dark hair, she waved to him as he continued on his way.

At the dairy stall, Señor Fuentes measured milk into Ramon's tin jug and counted out eggs. Beside him, his small son Felipe jumped excitedly up and down.

"Did you bring it, Ramon? Did you?"

Ramon chuckled and bent to hoist the boy up to the countertop.

"Of course I did. Did you think I'd forget?"

From a pocket Ramon took out his treasured wooden *boliche* and handed it to Felipe, who began immediately to swing the ball into the cup.

"Nine, ten, elev—Papá, Papá, look! I did nearly eleven! I'm getting better, aren't I?"

Señor Fuentes, carefully placing the eggs and milk into Ramon's basket, paused to pat his son on the head.

"What was it last time, seven? Soon you'll be ready for the championships." The shopkeeper tipped a wink at Ramon, who laughed, sharing the joke as he slipped the toy back into his pocket.

"See you next week." Ramon waved as he left the stall.

He crossed the busy street, keeping to the cool shadows of the shops that crowded the narrow way. Here in Juarez there were so many of the *adobe* buildings that they actually shaded the street!

Many of these places were *cantinas*, which Ramon did his best to steer clear of. Unlike the little ones back in Chihuahua, the *cantinas* here were serious trouble. With the revolutionary Madero exiled just over the border, political tensions were high, and gunfights were a frequent occurrence. Often the men Ramon saw slumped in the streets were not drunk, but dead.

He hurried past a newsstand, where a man wearing a gunbelt was urinating onto a poster of President Díaz. Good thing there were no *polícia* in sight, or they would arrest him. Would there really, wondered Ramon, be a war if Madero were to return to Mexico? And what would happen if—

"Stop him! Stop that boy! He stole my

wallet!"

Ramon froze, his heart pounding in his chest. *What? Me?*

For an awful moment, Ramon expected to feel a bullet thump into his back. Whirling around, he pressed himself against a cool *adobe* wall. What was happening?

It was the man from the newsstand. Hollering loudly, he snatched up his pants with one hand and brandished a pistol in the other as he lurched toward the horrified Ramon.

Then he was past. Popping off several wild shots, the angry man chased the real pickpocket, a starved and filthy boy, down the street until both were gone from sight. Several ruffians, sprawled in the dirt on the shaded side of the street and smoking cigarettes, looked up with mild interest, then returned to their card game.

Ramon's heartbeat gradually slowed to normal. What a close call. Chihuahua had *never* been this exciting! Taking a deep breath, he stepped away from the wall and continued on his way.

Later that evening, he could hear Tío Daniel's voice through the kitchen window as the family dined on the *patio*.

"Is it true what they are saying, that Díaz will be coming here?"

"*Sí*, Daniel. El Presidente is coming to Juarez to meet with the American president, Señor Taft."

This was interesting news. Ramon, eating beans and *tortillas* with his fingers while Luís snored on the kitchen floor beside him, strained to hear past the clink of silver and crystal outside as the conversation continued.

Díaz was going to meet with the American president. Here in Juarez! The meeting was to occur next week, he learned, at the bridge over the Rio Bravo. Ramon knew this bridge very well, having taken every opportunity to visit it. On its other side was the city of El Paso, Texas. *America*. One day soon Ramon would be crossing over that bridge himself, when Tío Daniel's cousin from New Mexico came for them.

On the day of the presidential visit, he knew, there would be many people come to watch. *And I will be there, too.*

What an occasion it would be. Ramon had read history books in school, and understood that a meeting like this would have great significance. For the first time ever, the presidents of both America and Mexico were coming together to talk. It was truly an historic event, one Ramon could someday tell his children and grandchildren about.

Tensions in the city escalated as the big day drew near. Mexican loyalists defended the president who had made them rich, while impoverished peasant folk openly mocked the tyrant who kept them poor. Ramon did his best to stay away from the fighting and waited eagerly for the big day to arrive.

People began gathering near the bridge before dawn. Restless murmurs rippled through the crowd. *Polícia* were everywhere, on the lookout for fights and arresting anyone who appeared to be making trouble.

For once Ramon was glad to be so small. He squirmed his way between people until he stood at the base of the bridge. From here he'd be able to see everything!

The presidents, he had learned, were to meet on the bridge, then proceed to El Paso, Texas, where they would have a brief conference. They would later return here to Juarez and go to the customhouse for a great banquet.

Ramon had watched in amazement all week as preparations were made at the customhouse. Trains with boxcars full of flowers arrived from the tropical south, along with shipments of household items from Díaz's presidential palace. Red velvet drapes, gold knives and crystal goblets, and even a great painting of George Washington, were only some of the treasures rumored to be gracing the opulent affair.

"Look! There he is!" called a voice from the crowd. The people went wild, some cheering and others angrily yelling. The men and women around Ramon began shoving each other as everyone suddenly tried to push to the front.

In all the confusion, Ramon missed seeing Díaz pass by. Vexed, he wormed through the crowd just in time to see El Presidente stop before a stout, well-dressed man who could only be America's president, William Taft.

The two men stood there facing each other. Ramon, from his place in the crowd, watched spellbound, his breath caught in amazement.

The simple suit Taft wore, fine as it was, couldn't compare with the dazzling elegance of Porfirio Díaz. In full military splendor, with the medals on his breast blindingly brilliant in the midday sun, El Presidente stood ramrod straight, the very image of a noble Mexican general.

Angry mutters from the crowd around Ramon reminded him that the Mexican military might soon be fighting its own poor people, and that the wealth of luxuries adorning the customhouse for the presidential banquet had come at the expense of the backbreaking labor of peasants like Ramon.

Now President Taft was smiling and extending his hand to Díaz. They would shake, and then continue on to their meeting in El Paso. But a gasp of horror rippled through the crowd. Something was wrong! Ramon craned his neck to see.

El Presidente was grasping his sword. Ramon stared in disbelief as Díaz slowly drew the weapon. Was he about to run it through the American president? Surely he would not do such a monstrous thing, here before all of these people!

Then Ramon let out his breath in relief, as did the rest of the crowd. El Presidente, ever the exhibitionist, was merely posturing. With military precision, he whipped out the sword and held it high in salute, standing stiffly at attention for a moment before lowering the weapon. With a deft motion he slid it back into its sheath, and then briskly accepted Taft's handshake. A moment later the two men were making their way down the other side of the bridge to El Paso.

Ramon stayed and watched until long after they had disappeared from view. The crowd gradually dispersed as the people returned to their activities, but Ramon remained where he was on the bridge, gazing at America on the other side.

He knew by now that much of what he had learned about America was inaccurate. Yes, some people lived in skyscrapers, but many more lived as he did, in small homes. Some

Americans were rich, but they had not started out this way. They worked hard, as he did, and many of them stayed poor all their lives.

From here on the bridge, over the surging Rio Bravo, or Rio Grande as the Americans called it, he could see El Paso. It looked much as Juarez did, hot, dusty, and crowded. Not at all the way he had imagined America to be. He wondered what the state of New Mexico would be like.

He did not have long to wait. Less than a week later a wagon arrived at the *casa*.

"Pancho! Welcome, welcome, how are you?" Tío Daniel warmly greeted his kinsman and ushered him inside out of the heat, gesturing for Rosa to bring them a pitcher of cool wine. The men talked all afternoon until everything was settled. Cousin Pancho would take them all to his *hacienda* in New Mexico the following day.

Ramon could hardly sleep that night.

"Do you suppose we'll be able to see a moving picture?" he asked Luís.

"I want to talk on a telephone!" was Luís's enthusiastic response.

"But we must remember," cautioned Ramon, "that we will be poor over there just as we are here. Just because there are modern things in America does not mean that Cousin Pancho's *hacienda* will have them."

Luís went silent, thinking about this. Then, in a timid voice, he asked, "But life in America will be better than here, right?"

"Of course it will!" Ramon was surprised Luís would even ask such a thing.

"How? If we're poor there then what is the difference?"

"The difference is that here in Mexico we will *always* be poor. What work is there for us to do? Labor in the fields all our lives? The rich people want the poor to stay poor so they can stay rich. Few common folk here have jobs that pay well."

"And in America, this is not so?" Luís was still confused.

"In America, people are kind and generous. They train you to do a job and then they pay you to do it." Ramon had learned that American children frequently grew up working in shops, mills, train stations, any place that needed extra help. Then, as adults, they often took over as managers.

"America is called the 'Land of Opportunity'," said Luís, stumbling a bit over the big word. "What does this mean?"

Ramon smiled and rolled over on the hard kitchen floor, snuggling his blanket close.

"It means there is hope."

THE fierce desert sun shone down on the clattering wagons as they turned onto the main avenue and made their noisy way up the bridge over the Rio Bravo. From the top of the bridge Ramon saw the city of El Paso, Texas, spreading out for miles. Beyond it, far beyond what he could see, was New Mexico and cousin Pancho's *hacienda.* It would be Ramon's new home. His American home.

He remembered what he had said to Luís. Hope. In America there would be hope. A chance for two young Mexican orphans to grow up and become American men.

Ramon knew it would likely be rough at first, toiling on the *hacienda.* But he had not forgotten the words of Señor Oaxaca: *I suspect that a bright boy like you can turn an opportunity such as this to your advantage.*

Work hard for your tío, *remember always the suffering of Jesus, and I have every confidence that one day you will achieve success.*

Oh yes, Ramon would work hard, and he suspected that there would be much suffering. But suffering could be endured, and he would keep a sharp watch for the chances he knew would come along. Someday he would live a life free of beatings and hunger. Maybe even raise a family.

He smiled at that. An American family.

Eagles circled high and free in the sky above, and the dry desert wind plucked at his shirt. He leaned back against the warm wooden side of the wagon as it began its descent toward El Paso. The bridge, with the mighty river surging beneath, seemed to be wishing him a farewell as the jingling horses led the wagon down the far side and into Texas.

With the cries of the eagles echoing above, he took a deep breath of sweet American air and entered his new home.

AUTHOR'S NOTE

The boy Ramon Ortiz really lived. He grew up to be my grandfather! The story you have just read was based on the notes that he wrote about his life. Soon these notes, both in English and in his original Spanish, may be available to read online.

Want to listen to Ramon's favorite song *Jesusita en Chihuahua*? Please visit

www.SycaMoorHomestead.com.

Lori Ortiz
April 2016